THE COEN BROTHERS

D1406610

THE COEN BROTHERS

THE STORY OF TWO AMERICAN FILMMAKERS

JOSH LEVINE

ECW PRESS

CANADIAN CATALOGUING IN PUBLICATION DATA

Levine, Josh
The Coen brothers : two American filmmakers

ISBN 1-55022-424-7

1. Coen, Joel. 2. Coen, Ethan. 3. Motion picture producers and directors –
United States – Biography. I. Title.

PN1998.3.C6635L48 2000   791.43'0233'092273   C00-931721-X

Cover and text design by Tania Craan
Layout by Mary Bowness
Front cover photo: Everett Collection
Back cover photo: Fox/Shooting Star
Printed by University of Toronto Press

Distributed in Canada by General Distribution Services,
325 Humber Blvd., Toronto, Ontario M9W 7C3

Published by ECW PRESS
2120 Queen Street East, Suite 200,
Toronto, Ontario, M4E 1E2
ecwpress.com

The publication of *The Coen Brothers* has been generously
supported by The Canada Council, the Ontario Arts Council,
and the Government of Canada through the Book Publishing
Industry Development Program. Canadä

PRINTED IN CANADA

TABLE OF CONTENTS

INTRODUCTION

THAT COEN BROTHERS
FEELING

"I just don't unnerstand it."
— Marge in *Fargo*

Oddly enough, my most vivid memory of a Coen brothers film is not actually of watching it, but of the moments immediately after.

It was the fall of 1991 and I was in New York on a visit. A friend and I had gone to see the recently released *Barton Fink*, and when it was over we stood on Fourteenth Street while the wind whipped garbage around our feet. My feelings about the film were just as tempestuous; I remember being both strangely exhilarated and angered by it, and having a desperate need to talk about what we had just seen. But at that moment, standing there, an awful chill went through me and the city seemed suddenly transformed. I was sure that at that very moment bizarre and terrible things were happening in all the city's apartments and seedy hotels and back alleys — that crazed writers were typing furiously, insanely intense grins on their faces; that serial killers were decapitating their victims;

that beds were turning into rivers of blood. It was as if the whole city had suddenly turned into the dreary and menacing Hotel Earle of the film.

Ah, that Coen brothers feeling.

I suppose this is a way of saying that my own feelings about the films of the Coen brothers are complicated, a messy combination of intellectual and emotional responses that don't easily resolve themselves into a simple statement. Yet there is no doubt I am a tremendous admirer of their work. Joel and Ethan Coen have written some of the most brilliantly funny, articulate, shocking — and sometimes morbid — American films of recent years. Their dialogue — from the terse, repressed emotions of *Blood Simple* to the absurd male banter in *The Big Lebowski* — is consistently alive and exciting. Their frequent monologues — from Hi's final dream of an idyllic future in *Raising Arizona* to Johnny Caspar's pained dissertation on the ethics of thieves in *Miller's Crossing* — are by turns thought-provoking and hilarious. Even their lowlife street thugs sound like undergraduate philosophy majors.

And the Coen brothers are not merely word-rich. Their talent is a rare combination of the literate and the visual. No doubt this is due to their collaborative approach, Ethan the more language-oriented, Joel the one who thinks in images. Their films are beautiful to look at, although not in a traditional way — not like lush Merchant-Ivory films, for example, with their love of Victorian "realism." No, the Coen brothers are more like abstract expressionists, making the screen into a moving cathedral of rising trees *(Miller's Crossing)*, a cityscape of idealized forms *(The Hudsucker Proxy)*, a white canvas of snow divided by a waving line of fence *(Fargo)*, or a symphony of pure shapes and neon colors *(The Big Lebowski)*. Often the camera eye itself imparts meaning as it tracks and swerves, giving us a God's-eye view of human weakness and stupidity.

For film buffs who know their genres and their directors, the films of the Coen brothers are a feast of clever references. The Coens have moved from the film-noir stylings of *Blood Simple* through the cartoon comedy of *Raising Arizona*, the gangster genre of *Miller's Crossing*, the Hollywood satire/horror film cross of *Barton Fink*, the antic 1940s-style comedy of *The Hudsucker Proxy*, the realistic thriller mode of *Fargo*, and on to the mystery/pothead combination of *The Big Lebowski*. They have parodied, commented on, embraced, subverted, and renewed each genre in turn, and a fan of the brothers can never be sure what style to expect next.

So why the mixed feelings, the hesitancy (not just my own, but of many crit-ics) to simply declare Joel and Ethan Coen among the great American filmmakers of our time? Perhaps it's because the brothers themselves have always refused to take themselves seriously, declaring that they hold to no film theory, have nothing significant to say, and that all they really want to do is have "fun." More likely it's the brothers' highly stylized approach, so much in oppo-sition to the "realism" of most American films. Most films say to the viewer: for two hours you are to believe these are real people, in a real place, leading real lives. The Coen brothers' films say: these seem like real characters, but look a lit-tle closer. Are they? This seems like a real place, but is it? Rarely does a film by the Coens simply allow us to accept it. Do we watch *Blood Simple* as a story of genuine jealousy, lust, and greed? Or do we see it, as Joel himself once said, as "phony" — a cleverly wrought mechanism, constructed according to the instructions encoded in the pulp novels and films of the past? Do we view the biker from hell in *Raising Arizona* as a manifestation of Hi's innermost fears of his own dark side, as a joking reference to the *Mad Max* movies, or merely as a hokey plot device? When we settle down comfortably with Marge and Norm at the end of *Fargo*, do we remember that the world is full of evil, incomprehensi-ble intention, or do we doubt the sincerity of even this, the Coen brothers' most "realistic" film?

Questions without easy answers. They don't, however, prevent us from being enthralled and entertained, from screaming and from laughing as we watch these films. Although I hope to offer some interesting and provocative ideas — ideas that sometimes come from the filmmaker's own words — this book is not intended to be an analysis of the films of the Coen brothers. Let's leave that to the academics. Instead, it is the story of the making of Joel and Ethan's films. It is about where the brothers came from, how they got started, how the screen-plays get written, and the films get shot. It is about raising money, about maintaining the integrity of independence, about reviews good and bad, about box-office failure and success. It is full of nuggets of information, some trivial, some significant, all, I hope, interesting and entertaining. It is the story of Joel and Ethan Coen and the life of making movies.

CHAPTER ONE

SIBERIA, U.S.A.

OR, HOW TO GROW UP JEWISH IN MINNESOTA

"We'll hear from that kid. And I don't mean a postcard."
— Maury in *Barton Fink*

The Two-Minute Trailer

In 1981, if you happened to be rich, a contributor to Jewish charities, and living in Minnesota, chances are good that at some time a thin young man with long hair managed to talk his way into your office or, even worse, your living room. He introduced himself as Joel Coen, a hometown boy from a good family who wanted to make a feature film with his even younger brother, Ethan. You might have been impressed by his confidence, his academic parents, the degrees from New York University (Joel) and Princeton (Ethan). And if you let him stay for even five minutes he would already be setting up a 16-mm projector, lowering the lights, and shining two minutes of film on your office or living-room wall.

The film showed gunshots piercing a wall and light filtering through the holes.

It showed a man being buried alive.

1

This, Joel explained, was only the trailer. The film had yet to be made. The Coen brothers were looking for investors — they needed a mere three-quarters of a million dollars — and felt sure you would want to be one.

"What is the film about?" you might have asked. Adultery, came the reply from the nice young man. Double-crossing. Suspicion. Murder. And it all took place in Texas. "Have you got a track record? Have you made any other films?" No, came the answer from the nice young man. But, he said with modest pride, I did work as an editor on a film. "And what was it called?" *The Evil Dead.*

Chances are you wished the young man well and ushered him out the door with some relief. But if you didn't — if some gut feeling caused you to nod your head and take out your checkbook — then for a mere ten thousand dollars you bought yourself a ticket to film history.

The trailer that Joel Coen schlepped around with him to show investors had been shot during the President's Day long weekend of 1981 as a promotional tool. Making it had been the suggestion of Robert Tapert, who had also worked on the low-budget *The Evil Dead*, a film that would be declared an instant classic and go on to draw millions of dollars from the pockets of horror-hungry cinema-goers. In fact, Sam Raimi, the writer/director of *The Evil Dead* and an important influence on the Coen brothers, had used just such a trailer to raise *his* money.

At the shoot were Joel, Ethan, Barry Sonnenfeld, whom Joel had met at NYU and who was acting as cinematographer, and Sonnenfeld's cousin, a neuropharmacologist, who had been arm-twisted to be the focus puller. None of the young filmmakers had ever before used a 35-mm camera — the kind used by *real* feature-filmmakers — but shooting over the long weekend meant that they could use the rented camera and lights from Thursday to Tuesday and only pay for one day. Afterwards, Joel, Ethan, and Barry screened the footage together. Still inexperienced, and anxiety-ridden by nature, Sonnenfeld was nervous to learn what the brothers thought of the results; but when they offered no compliments, he felt crushed. It would be some time before he realized that the Coens were just too emotionally reticent to show how excited they were by what they saw on the screen.

Armed with the trailer — reduced to 16-mm after Joel discovered how hard it was to get investors to go to a theater to see it — Joel headed back to

Minnesota. For raising money, there was nothing like being a kid from the neighborhood. As for Ethan, he stayed in New York, working as a typist at Macy's (a job the literate young man liked to compare to that of Bartleby in the famous Melville story) to support the two of them. Joel met with a fundraiser for Hadassah, the Jewish charitable organization that raises millions of dollars each year, and came out with a list of the 100 wealthiest Jews in the state. Then he started knocking on doors. As their father, Edward Coen, remembered, "They were very, very worried when they were making *Blood Simple*. Everything would turn on that, and they realized it. But when they were raising money, they would walk in and seem very calm." As for Joel, with no real track record and nothing to show but two minutes of film, he felt as if he were "selling air."

Usually filmmakers trying to raise money hire a broker who in turn approaches investors. But brokers usually hit up people who already have a knowledge of investing in film — people unlikely to take a chance on untested newcomers like the Coens. This campaign instead saw inexperienced film investors being approached by Joel, the even more inexperienced fundraiser. In the pitch, he tried to be as straightforward as possible. Each investor had to put up ten to twenty thousand dollars for a share in the film. Because it would be a limited partnership, the investors would have no power over the film itself; the Coen brothers would have complete control. While there was certainly a chance the money would never be recovered, it was also possible that with foreign distribution rights, pay-TV, and video-cassette sales the investors might actually see a profit.

For every twenty people he went to see, Joel managed to convince one. Doctors, lawyers, architects, even a beauty-salon owner came on board; often they were self-made men and women with an entrepreneurial spirit and a willingness to take risks. They were impressed by the brothers' readiness to assume a large risk themselves; the Coens would not be paid a cent until the investors began to see a profit. One of them was a man named Daniel Bacaner, who became not only an investor but also the film's executive producer and a useful provider of introductions to other potential partners. Joel and Ethan's parents even kicked in some money. In the end, it took the brothers nine months to raise the necessary $750,000.

The first step was over. Now all they had to do was make the film, which the brothers had titled *Blood Simple*. Later Ethan would say, "Every little step, considered one at a time, is not terribly daunting." A good thing, too, as it would be three more years before the film even reached theaters.

Utterly Suburban

By the time the Coen brothers were born (Joel on November 29, 1954, Ethan on September 21, 1957), the St. Louis Park suburb of Minneapolis had about 30,000 residents living in its ten square miles. Envisioned as a boomtown in the late nineteenth century, this former farmland (the name came from the St. Louis Railroad) emerged as something more sedate — a bedroom community for people working in the city. It has five synagogues, and, if one of Ethan's fantastical short stories can be believed, the boys attended a nearby Hebrew school and helped raise money to plant trees in Israel. On the other hand, there don't seem to have been many Jewish families on their particular street. Frances McDormand, the actress whom the brothers would discover and who would later marry Joel, said: "They grew up pretty isolated as the only Jewish kids around and they're pretty big on loyalty and dependability." As for which has been the greater influence — the fact that the Coen brothers are Jewish or the fact that they are Minnesotans — well, the films leave much room for debate.

Their father, Edward, was an economics professor at the University of Minnesota. "There wasn't much back then to suggest that anything [special] would happen" to his kids, he later said. Rena, their mother, was a professor of fine arts at St. Cloud State University. Although neither parent has claimed any influence over them, it is possible that the brothers developed their strong visual imagination from their mother and their financial savvy from their father. A sister, Debbie, was the oldest. Later she would become a doctor and move to Israel. Her brothers, however, refused to even visit Israel, saying that they imagined it to be like "armed Jewish summer camp." Otherwise, Debbie is not much mentioned by Ethan and Joel and it is tempting to turn once again to that same short story by Ethan: "I saw almost nothing of my sister from the onset of her puberty until she left for college six years later. She spent those years in the bathroom washing her hair."

A couple of bright kids, Joel and Ethan both found school, and suburban Minnesotan life, boring. They wiled away some of the cold and snowy

Minnesota winters skiing. Ethan liked to write even in elementary school, and once wrote a play with a school friend about King Arthur. His talent for humor was already emerging; when the king is about to leave the castle, his nurse calls out to him, "Don't forget to put on a sweater." One year the brothers started a newspaper, *The Flag Street Sentinel*, which sold for two cents a copy, showing early on their financial initiative. The paper, however, only lasted for two issues.

Mostly they just hung around the house and watched television. "Utterly suburban" is how they later described their childhood years. Joel even pointed to this dullness as an ironic source for the strangeness and violence of their films: "It's to compensate for the fact that our lives were incredibly mundane. We grew up in a typically middle-class family in the United States' equivalent of Siberia. All that cold weather drives you inside to watch movies." Like many of their contemporaries, they had, as a friend put it, "fantastically overgrown hair" although Joel's grew down and Ethan's grew frizzy. Joel was the more gregarious of the two and often had friends over while Ethan, described by his mother as "very quiet, very reticent," often made himself content with a book, a taste he would never outgrow.

Being three years apart in age, and often in different schools, the brothers (who call each other "Joe" and "Eth") didn't spend that much time together as they grew up — even though they shared a room. Ethan has said, "We certainly have more to do with each other now than we ever did when we were under the same roof." One thing they did share, however, was a love of movies, most of which they saw on television. One late-night movie show on a local Minneapolis station showed a lot of Italian pictures, everything from high art (Fellini) to lowbrow *(Sons of Hercules)*. The brothers lapped it all up, which may be the source of their own mixture of low- (horror films) and high-art aesthetics. They also loved Tarzan movies, Jerry Lewis comedies, and anything with Bob Hope or Tony Curtis or Doris Day. In fact, it might well be that all of that television-watching was the biggest influence of all. It spurred them on to their first adventures in filmmaking.

In an attempt to relieve the boredom of lounging around the Coens' basement den with nothing to do, a kid named Ron Neter (who would grow up to be a commercial producer in L.A.) came up with the idea of buying a movie camera. The only problem was motivating Joel to earn enough money by mowing neighborhood lawns. But Joel came through and made enough to purchase a Vivitar Super-8 camera. Maybe it was the fact that the camera was bought with Joel's money that made him the director.

Their first experiment was simply to film the television screen — a hint, perhaps, of their later tendency to make postmodern, self-referential films? The second was to film their own feet as they went down a playground slide — future wild camera moves? Then they got the idea of doing remakes of films they had seen on television. Needing an actor, they roped in a neighbor named Mark Zimering, nicknamed Zeimers. (He grew up to become a research physician.) Thus Cornell Wilde's *The Naked Prey* became *Zeimers in Zambezi*, in which Ethan also appeared, a native brandishing a spear and wearing black-rimmed glasses. Showing early on their ability to stretch a special-effects budget, they simulated a parachute drop by filming a plane going overhead, then a miniature parachute floating down, then a boy actor hitting the ground on a white sheet.

"We'd see something on TV and round up our friends the next day to film it," Joel recounted. Ethan remembered that their films were "really cheesy and didn't look very good." There was *Ed . . . a Dog*, a remake, or rather a reinterpretation of the 1943 classic *Lassie Come Home*, with Zeimers in a Cub Scout uniform and a yarmulke; Ethan, playing the mother, wore his sister Debbie's tutu in order to get into the role. They even remade Otto Preminger's *Advise and Consent*, a film which they never actually saw.

But not all the films were remakes. There were originals like *Henry Kissinger — Man on the Go* and *Lumberjacks of the North*, a movie that, like *Fargo* decades later, used their cold northern upbringing as source material. (Actually, the inspiration for the film was the fact that both Ethan and Joel owned plaid shirts.) Their nascent contempt for realism can be seen in a scene in which the lumberjack pulls a pancake, already dripping with syrup, from his pocket. And finally there was *The Banana Film*, which included the Coens' first of many depictions of vomiting. In this one Zeimers tipped out a mixture of ketchup and bananas.

These early films are amusing, but they are probably more important than they might first seem. It is just this sort of young ambition that can mature into a serious avocation. Many famous filmmakers began just this way, by making amateurish Super-8 movies in which they first learned what the results of translating "life" to film might look like. While the equipment was simple and the stories adolescent, the process was not really so very different from professional filmmaking if one considers that all artistic creation is a kind of play. As for the Coens, they were already showing a tendency to draw on other "real" movies for their own inspiration. As Joel himself has said, "We've been dicking around cameras since we were young. Things aren't really so different now. The camera just got bigger."

In high school, Joel was an average student, never really aspiring to academic excellence. Motivated by a combination of boredom and a claustrophobic sense of the restrictions of Minnesota, he asked his parents if he might change schools. They sent him to Simon's Rock in Great Barrington, Massachusetts. Founded in 1966, Simon's Rock was the only school in the United States that allowed students to begin taking college courses during what would normally be their high school years. Students were expected to be mature, motivated, and self-disciplined, and to pursue their own interests with independent study — just the right sort of environment for a smart but uninspired student like Joel.

Not surprisingly, Ethan followed Joel's example and also went to Simon's Rock. In fact, years later the school would proudly feature not Joel but Ethan by putting the cover of his first book of stories on its web site. But, as would happen so often in the future, the older brother paved the way for the younger, setting his life on course alongside his own. Their relationship, however, is not as one-sided as that; as Joel seems to realize, he needs his younger brother as much as Ethan needs him. Each can fulfill his goals only with the help of the other.

College Boys

Never one to put his academic career first, Joel missed the application deadline for most of the universities that he might have gone on to after Simon's Rock. One school that had a later deadline was New York University and so Joel chose it by default. Finding a ground-floor apartment on the Upper West Side, Joel settled into the city that would become his permanent home. The four years he spent in the undergraduate film program at NYU (a school renowned for producing such alumni as Martin Scorsese and Oliver Stone, but whose prestige resides more in its graduate program), were desultory ones. Joel would sit at the back of the class and make sarcastic remarks under his breath. He did have to make films, however, including a 30-minute thesis film. Joel's was called *Soundings* and while its story doesn't directly relate to any of the later films, it does show a characteristic mix of drama and uneasy humor, not to mention a certain offbeat sexuality. In the film a woman engaged in sex with her deaf boyfriend verbally fantasizes about screwing the boyfriend's best friend who just happens to be listening in the next room.

During Joel's first year at NYU, Ethan was still at Simon's Rock. Every so often Joel would visit his brother on the weekend and pester Ethan about making an independent film together. They had no actual idea for a film, never mind a script, but Joel already had the desire and ambition to do it.

Graduating from Simon's Rock, Ethan, who was more interested in studying than his brother, had the good sense to get his applications in on time. Princeton accepted him and he went off to do an undergraduate degree in philosophy. But while he was the more bookish and intellectual one of the brothers, he too doesn't seem to have taken university too seriously. Asked about studying philosophy, he later simply said that he went to Princeton "for fun" — a goal he certainly achieved the time when, after taking a term off school, he didn't bother to notify the registrar that he was returning. Realizing his mistake, Ethan tried to "fix" it by presenting a fake doctor's note saying that he had lost an arm in a hunting accident in his brother-in-law's living room. Less than amused, the school asked him to see a psychiatrist.

Whatever success the brothers might have anticipated, it was clearly not going to be in academia. Joel did make one more stab at it, however, enrolling in the graduate program of the film school at the University of Texas. His reasons, however, had little to do with a desire for more classes: Joel was following a woman. He spent nine months there, but whether or not this woman was the same woman he soon married has never been made public. In any case, Joel did marry during these early years, but the relationship quickly ended in divorce. It was an amicable parting, however, and made easier by the fact that neither party had any money.

Joel ended up back in New York where Ethan now came to join him after his own graduation. Joel had already begun to pick up some film work in the city. He was hired on as a crew member, usually production assistant (or PA), on industrial and sponsored films. One film had the exciting title *How To Buy a Used Car*, although it would probably be stretching things to suggest that the seed for the car-salesman character in *Fargo* was planted here. He also worked on some music videos. One of the people who hired Joel was his NYU friend Barry Sonnenfeld. "He was the world's worst PA," Sonnenfeld later remembered. "He got three parking tickets, came late, set fire to the smoking machine."

Joel seemed to have more talent for editing, work he managed to get on some low-budget horror films. He landed one job in 1980 as an assistant editor, before even meeting the writer/director. Their auspicious introduction took place on a New York sidewalk in front of the rented cutting room, as Joel stood waiting for a 22-year-old independent filmmaker named Sam Raimi to appear. Sure enough, up pulled the station wagon, loaded with cans of film and a rather nervous Raimi, who had never driven in New York before. The first thing that Raimi saw was "this guy . . . with long scraggly hair down to his chest, looking undernourished. I thought he was trying to rip us off."

The meeting of these two odd young men would prove to be the most important connection — and friendship — the Coen brothers would ever make. For it was the example of Sam Raimi that showed them the way for their own first film. And it is impossible to continue the story of the Coen brothers without pausing to give a brief portrait of a young man who was, if anything, even more obsessed with movies than they were.

Sam Raimi's Theater of Blood

Born in 1960 to a Royal Oak, Michigan, family in retailing, Raimi began making Super-8 movies with a junior-high classmate, Bruce Campbell, who would eventually star in *The Evil Dead*. He also began collecting comic books, accumulating thousands of titles; he enjoyed them in part because they seemed like "visual, storyboarded films." Raimi spent all his available money making movies, even when he eventually enrolled at Michigan State University. To make *The Evil Dead*, his first feature — the raw footage was what he brought to Manhattan in that station wagon — Raimi raised a half-million dollars with the help of a half-hour preview film to sell the investors. Working with two old friends, Campbell and Robert Tapert, whom he met at Michigan U, Raimi shot the film in Tennessee as well as in his own garage. Filmed in 16-mm, the film had to be blown up to 35, resulting in a somewhat grainy look.

Gore with style: Sam Raimi on the set of *Evil Dead II*
PHOTOFEST

It is fair to say that Raimi, despite having a visual flair and an unstoppable determination, did not show the budding genius that the Coen brothers would in their first, far more audacious feature. *The Evil Dead* is a cheap horror film that does not rise above its genre. Borrowing its plot from *Night of the Living Dead*, among others, stealing scenes from *The Exorcist*, *The Texas Chainsaw Massacre*, *Carrie*, and elsewhere, it tells the story of five young men and women who go to an isolated cabin and discover a Book of the Dead. Dormant spirits in the nearby woods awaken and begin to take possession of the characters; they can be destroyed only by gruesome dismemberment. The script is wooden, the characters have no distinguishing qualities, and the amateurish acting does nothing to breathe any life into them. The violence is intended to thrill and shock, and, despite the sometimes cheesy effects, it does. One could easily argue that the film exploits an adolescent audience's lowest impulses; one young woman's possession, for example, is nothing more than a supernatural rape scene. Sex-tinged, gratuitous violence — is there an easier way to bring in an audience?

But the film does have a certain style, especially in its restless camera movements (for example, skirting just above the ground) which Raimi employed without the use of any expensive equipment and which likely influenced Joel's own predilection for unusual camera movements. The occasional shot — a car's headlights cutting through the gloom of night, for instance — seems to prefigure some in *Blood Simple*. There is, however, an underlying tongue-in-cheek humor that redeems it somewhat; the humor comes from the absurdity of the gore, making the audience laugh even while feeling revolted. Violence in films by the Coen brothers often has a similar effect. Without question, the Coens, who have expressed nothing but admiration for Raimi's work, learned some lessons in surprising and horrifying audiences from his horror films. The final sequence in *Blood Simple*, in which Visser's hand is pinned to the windowsill by a knife, may well have been inspired by a knife-holding severed hand in *The Evil Dead*.

But the most important lesson that Joel learned from Sam Raimi is that an absolutely determined person, no matter how young or unconnected to Hollywood, could still make a feature film. It took money, but not millions; ingenuity and hard work could compensate for a small budget. And an independent filmmaker could keep control of his film, unlike Hollywood directors who were subject to the whims of their studios.

Raimi's picture did not actually get released until after the Coens' own movie, *Blood Simple*, was already in the can, but this is as good a place as any to record the rest of the story. After having difficulty finding a distributor, Raimi used a rave review by horror novelist Stephen King, who saw it at the Cannes Film Festival ("the most ferociously original horror film of 1982," he said), to land a distributor. The film grossed $1 million within two weeks of its U.S. opening; in New York lines stretched around the block. The *New York Times'* Vincent Canby even wrote a think-piece about it. Sam Raimi made money for his investors and put himself on the map.

Joel worked on two other low-budget horror films, *Fear No Evil* (released in 1981) and one called *Nightmare*, from which he was understandably fired after declaring that the footage was too incoherent to be edited into a film. But while he was working as an editor and Ethan was slaving at Macy's, the brothers had begun to write scripts together. On Ethan's arrival in New York they moved in together to an apartment on Riverside Drive on the West Side. There they would lounge about or take turns sitting at the typewriter, or, in the case of

Ethan, pace restlessly about. They wrote a script called *Coast to Coast*, a screw-ball comedy (the brothers tended to think in old-fashioned genres) in which the communist Chinese were cloning an army of Einsteins. They wrote a script for an independent producer based on a treatment that the producer already owned. It too never went anywhere. They wrote another called *Suburbicon* and managed to sell it to another producer, only to see it go nowhere, although as late as 1998 they spoke of returning to the script and making it themselves.

Still, they wrote, often treating it as a game and setting up exercises for themselves that must have reminded them of their games as kids. On one occasion they went to Central Park and commanded themselves to write a ten-minute movie in ten minutes. They preferred to eat in the most unpretentious New York restaurants — the Woolworth's lunch counter or Harvey's — so that they could eavesdrop on conversations that might help them write dialogue. Michael Miller, an editor who later worked on *Raising Arizona*, said that many of the opening lines of *Blood Simple* were overheard by the brothers in New York.

Because Joel and Ethan hit it off so well with Sam Raimi, who could bring to the more diffident brothers some of the energy and drive they needed to get a career going, the three of them decided to try and write together. Raimi found himself amazed by the synchronicity of the brothers, the way they seemed to complete each other's thoughts. "Writing with them was like watching a badminton game," he said. "Joel would mention a line of dialogue and Ethan would finish the sentence. Then Joel would say the punch line, and Ethan would type it up." When the words didn't come, they'd pace the apartment, one following the other.

Raimi decided to put down some money and actually hired the brothers to help him write a sort of comic film-noir parody which he called *The XYZ Murders*. The film would eventually get made and released (more on this later), but the brothers never seemed to invest as much personal stake in it as Raimi himself, and when all three later disavowed it, Joel and Ethan took the experience rather good-naturedly as just another lesson in the dangers of handing over control to the big studios.

For now, however, the brothers didn't seem to be getting anywhere. Joel had worked on enough independent films to realize that the best — maybe the only — way to get a first film made was to do it yourself. He had been pestering Ethan long enough. Now it was time to stop talking and take the plunge.

CHAPTER TWO

PULP FICTION

BLOOD SIMPLE

"Now in Russia, they got it all mapped out so that everyone pulls for everyone else — that's the theory, anyway. But what I know about is Texas . . ." — Opening voice-over, *Blood Simple*

Joel and Ethan knew that a genre film would be the easiest to sell to a distributor, and besides, they had always thought in genres, even as far back as their Super-8 film days. They had no desire, however, to go the horror-movie route, as relatively easy as that seemed. For them, even at the beginning, the script took on a far greater importance than the horror genre had room for. This emphasis on the screenplay may well have been the influence of the younger Ethan, who had liked writing from a young age and was a voracious reader. In fact, Joel may have wanted to drag his brother into filmmaking because he knew that without Ethan's talent with language he himself might not be able to write a successful script. Joel had always thought visually, in images. While this was not only useful but absolutely necessary for a good director, it alone couldn't produce a script.

In deciding what kind of film to write, the brothers didn't

draw so much on their film knowledge as on their liking for popular fiction. A trio of crime writers has hovered over their own imaginations like guardian angels from the very beginning: Dashiell Hammett, Raymond Chandler, and James M. Cain. Hard-boiled writers, each of them could write cutting, witty, street-smart dialogue and could surprise the reader with their plot machinations. Later, the brothers would draw more directly from Hammett and Chandler, but this first time out it was the ghost of James M. Cain that came to the forefront. They had read his books a few years earlier when they had been reissued in paperback; Ethan and Joel were not above "borrowing" plots and even characters when it suited them, and Cain's *Double Indemnity* (made into a movie with a script by Chandler) and *The Postman Always Rings Twice* certainly provided material for them here. The lethal triangle of husband, wife, and lover, for instance, came straight from Cain's novels. The title, however, came from Hammett's novel *Red Harvest*; he coined it to convey the state of confusion that plagues a murderer after he has killed, causing him to make mistakes.

Although most films noirs and crime novels are set in major cities, Ethan and Joel decided to play with the form by setting theirs in the rural countryside of Texas. Likely they also realized that it would be easier — and cheaper — to film there, just as Raimi had filmed in Tennessee. What did they actually know about Texas? Nothing except what Joel had seen during his nine months of graduate school there. And what he loved was the "gothic, mythic, overblown, overheated" quality of the place. Besides, neither Ethan nor Joel subscribed to the old rule that a writer should write about what he knows. If anything, they had more confidence in what they could invent, in large part because they saw writing a film as a kind of complex game rather than an attempt to draw painful personal truths from one's inner soul. This is what Joel meant when he later said, "We had absolutely nothing to lose and nothing better to do. And we never looked at it as a career. It's just a 'phony' movie anyway." By "phony" he meant that it was taken not from real life but from books and other films.

Joel also said, "The attraction of a genre is that the audience comes to it with a set of rules and expectations. The fun comes from circumventing the rules and putting a new spin on the genre." It might have been a construct, but the brothers let themselves have fun constructing it. Their approach was that by entertaining themselves, they had a shot at entertaining the audience, which in their opinion was the primary purpose of any movie. (More deliberately artistic independent filmmakers, of course, might disagree; this too makes the Coens different.) The character of the private detective as a destructive force was new, as was the importation from another genre, the horror movie, of elements like plot surprises and the shocking quality of the violence. This cross-fertilization of genres would become a Coen specialty, as would the layering of uneasy laughter over scenes that seemed anything but funny. Bringing in humor, however, was something they had seen their literary idols, Hammett, Chandler, and Cain, do, not to mention Alfred Hitchcock, with his suspense/horror thrillers.

And so they began to write during the evenings and weekends of 1980, using as settings the roadhouses, bars, and stretches of desolate highway that Joel had seen in Texas. Opting for a plan to not plan — which they would continue to use — they eschewed an outline and simply started from the beginning, writing each scene in order. When they came to a turning point in the plot, they tried to take the script in the most unusual and unexpected direction. The better typist of the two, Ethan did most of the finger work, although sometimes Joel took a turn. Unlike some writing partners, who write their scenes separately and then bring them together, the brothers always worked side by side. Often ideas and words didn't come and they would just mope around the apartment, take naps, and smoke a lot of Camel cigarettes. Ethan would pace. Joel would stretch out on the couch. And then suddenly there would be a burst of writing.

The brothers felt it was somehow right to open with a short voice-over monologue, something they would also do in future films. Avoided by most contemporary screenwriters, voice-overs have something of an antiquated feel to them. But Joel and Ethan liked evoking a "voice" reminiscent of the narrative voice that shapes a novel, and also appreciated the sense of storytelling that it helped to set up for the audience. For the most part, though, they gave the script a kind of omniscient point of view, which allows the audience to know more of the truth than any of the characters.

In writing *Blood Simple*, Ethan and Joel drew not only on Cain but on other films too. The murder of the husband, Marty, was based on one in Hitchcock's *Torn Curtain*. In the Hitchcock film it took ten minutes of screen time to kill one of the characters; Joel and Ethan decided that Marty would last twice that long. And the film's climactic ending borrows both from *Psycho* and from Fritz Lang's *Ministry of Fear*.

When Sam Raimi made *The Evil Dead* he was happy to settle for whatever young actors he could convince to be in his movie. But from the very beginning the Coen brothers took a different approach. Although Joel would develop a reputation for *not* being much of an actor's director — mostly because he and Ethan aren't always terribly interested in the actors' creative suggestions — the brothers understood from the beginning that actors were more than just window dressing. They breathed life into the lines that the screenwriters wrote; their faces, gestures, and actions brought meaning to a film that words couldn't even begin to suggest. The simple truth is that just as you can't bake a good cake without good ingredients, you can't make a good film without good actors. Even as they were writing, Joel and Ethan were thinking about who might play the roles. Of course they had no reason to believe that an actor with a real career would want to be in a film by a couple of young upstarts with no reputation and a pathetically limited budget. But why should that stop them from dreaming, especially since the sort of actors they were interested in were not A-list Hollywood stars but character actors whose names were likely not known even by audiences who had seen them in dozens of movies? In *Blood Simple*, the role they felt was the real linchpin was that of the evil private detective, the smirking and amoral hired shamus who protected his own interests rather than his clients and who was not above murder to make a few dollars. Joel and Ethan thought the role would be best played by M. Emmet Walsh, a character actor whose work they had particularly admired in the Dustin Hoffman film *Straight Time*. They even found it easier to write the role by imagining Walsh playing it.

Writing Blood Simple

The story that Joel and Ethan came up with was more intricately plotted and suspenseful than any of their subsequent films would be until *Fargo*. Although their later tendency was to write long and convoluted speeches for their characters, here the exchanges were, with few exceptions, usually one or two lines. But even in this earliest film the Coen brothers' fondness for characters with metaphysical tendencies and a liking for rhetorical flourishes can be seen in a few places like the private investigator's references to Russia or Marty the cuckolded husband's mention of the ancient Greek practice of beheading the messenger who brought bad news. Marty's confession to Abby — "In here I'm anal," while pointing to his head — shows that at the very least he's been dipping into the magazines at the doctor's office to get some secondhand Freud. And some of the incidental speech, such as the evangelist on the radio while Ray drives through the night with the supposedly dead Marty in the backseat (". . . it's my belief that this Antichrist is alive today and livin' somewhere in Europe, in that ten-nation alliance I spoke of . . ."), gives the brothers a little more room to play.

At the start of the screenplay, Abby is being driven through a night rainstorm by Ray, an employee at Abby's husband Marty's strip bar. She is leaving Marty, but instead of driving to Houston, Ray and Abby end up having sex in a motel. Unfortunately for them, their photographs are taken by a private investigator (the character they envisioned being played by M. Emmet Walsh), who then takes them to Marty. At this point comes one of the film's most memorable lines of dialogue, when the private investigator responds to the photographs by referring to the Greek practice of beheading the messenger. "Well, gimme a call when you wanna cut off my head," the PI chuckles. "I can crawl around without it."

Marty's suffering over his lost wife might have been played for sympathy, but the Coens insert a scene in which, just after seeing the photos, he tries to bully a woman at the bar into a night out with him. Of course this aggressiveness can be read back to his pain and jealousy, but it certainly makes him less than appealing. In fact, in the original script, the conversation runs longer and is played more for laughs. The seed for later events is planted when Ray comes to see Marty to get the two weeks of pay he's owed and Marty warns Ray to beware of Abby two-timing *him*.

As written, Ray is a simple character, more a victim of other people's actions than a master of his own. Abby seems to have more passion, but it is easy to see how the actors will have to work to evoke the audience's sympathy for the characters. Marty sneaks into Ray's house and tries to kidnap Abby; in the script the attack seems to be more of a rape, but the Coens, who will turn out to be far more reticent about showing sex, sexual violence, or nudity than straight violence, played this down in the shooting. Abby gets away by breaking his finger and then kicking him in the testicles, and so Marty becomes the first of many Coen characters to undergo a succession of humiliations and assaults upon his body. Marty hires the private investigator — whose name in the script notes,

"Loren Visser," is never actually spoken in the film — to kill both her and Ray.

The private investigator does indeed sneak up once more on Abby and Ray in bed, but he shoots them with his camera instead of his gun, doctoring the photographs to look like they have been murdered. Presenting the photos to Marty in his office, where Marty gets sick to his stomach for the second time in the script, the private investigator then pulls out Abby's gun, which he has stolen, and shoots Marty in the chest. It seems that it is easier to kill Marty and then leave Abby's gun for the police to find than it would have been to cover up the lovers' deaths and leave Marty alive to go "simple" and spill the beans.

It is at this point in the script that the omniscient view of the camera, which the audience shares, really comes into play. We know what Ray doesn't when he comes to Marty's office and finds him dead — that he is making a mistake in thinking that it was Abby who killed him. Disaster follows, all as a result of this error, as, in a long, wordless sequence, Ray tries to dispose of the body. This sequence, perhaps the most talked-about part of the film, uses some of the horror tropes that Joel learned from Sam Raimi and others; the dead that will not stay dead, the hand that suddenly reaches out to grasp the hero, the burial of the still-moving body. But unlike those cheap horror films that pile one thrill onto another, the Coens use darkness, tension, and the slow building of fear in a far more effective way. And the whole sequence, carefully constructed during the writing stage, had a larger narrative purpose. By choosing to perform these malevolent acts, Ray is in effect emotionally committing himself to Abby, who he thinks, wrongly, had been the one to shoot Marty. This is why Ray stops at a gas station afterwards to phone Abby and say, "I love you." He has just helped Abby kill her husband; how could he have done such a thing if not for love? He *must* love her.

And that is why, during their confused conversation in Abby's apartment (confused because Ray thinks Abby shot Marty and Abby thinks that Ray did something to Marty but doesn't know what) Ray says, "What's important is that we did it. That's the only thing that matters. We both did it for each other. . . ." Clearly he is groping for some kind of salvation that his intuition tells him can only come from love. But when Abby says, "What are you talkin' about, Ray? I haven't done anything funny" — the very words that Marty told Ray Abby would one day say when she was lying to him — he suddenly loses faith in the flimsy salvation he has tried to construct for himself.

Actor M. Emmet
Walsh told the
brothers to cut the
"sophomoric stuff"
GLOBE PHOTOS

Meanwhile, Abby's own doubts about Ray begin to grow. She visits Marty's office and discovers bloodstains; then she has a dream — the brothers will often include dreams in their scripts — in which Marty, come back to life, appears in her apartment only to bend over and vomit blood in a terrible gush. (Poor Marty; even dead, he must suffer indignities.)

The film's climactic sequence finds Abby discovering Ray in her apartment. They argue over whether to keep the lights on or not; Ray is fearful of something looking into the big windows from outside, while Abby is now afraid of Ray. Only the audience knows that the private investigator is across the road with a rifle; he shoots through the window, killing Ray. What follows is a cat-and-mouse game between Abby and the private investigator, who breaks in — with the ironic touch that Abby thinks the murderous intruder is Marty. When the PI reaches his hand out one window and into another, in the room where Abby is, she stabs his hand with a knife, pinning it to the sill. Now comes the neat visual moment that the brothers would include in the fundraising trailer, as Visser fires through the wall between the rooms, letting in shafts of light.

Then, like some horror-film monster who will not stop, he breaks his fist through the wall and pulls out the knife pinning his other hand to the sill. The sequence — and the film — will not end until Abby shoots him through a door and Visser, realizing she thinks he is Marty, offers his amoral, anarchic laugh one last time. And the very last moment, envisioned in the script and fulfilled later in the shooting, is an odd little joke, as the dying Visser, sprawled beneath the bathroom sink, watches a single drop of water gather on the pipes above his head and start to fall.

Of all their scripts, *Blood Simple* shows the greatest influence of its sources, in this case James M. Cain. The mechanics of the clever plot take precedence over characters and ideas, and unlike in their later scripts, the silences carry as much weight as the dialogue. The motivations behind the plot come straight out of pulp-fiction conventions — lust, jealousy, greed. In most ways, *Blood Simple* will prove to be the Coens' least personal script. (By personal I don't mean autobiographical; none of their films is that. I mean a script that is allowed to dwell on their personal interests, whether intellectual, visual, or of some other kind.) And yet it is by no means without originality. The plot, though a variation on the age-old lovers' triangle, finds a new way to play it out. And the characters, although sketched in briefly and mostly, in good old Aristotelian fashion, by their actions, all have something new about them. The betrayed husband is made sick with his emotional pain. The lover can only explain his actions through love. The private investigator, rather than being a neutral observer or even the hero, as in much pulp fiction, turns out to be the embodiment of anarchy and amorality. The wife abandons one love for another, but in the end must fight to survive on her own. Whatever life lessons might be drawn from the script are chilling ones: the truth is unknowable by any one person; love cannot save us; in the end we fight the demons alone.

Getting Ready

So the brothers finished their script and, with Barry Sonnenfeld as the cinematographer, shot their two-minute promotional trailer. Sonnenfeld, who had met Joel at NYU, was a graduate of the university's more prestigious Graduate Institute of Film and Television. Born in New York in 1953 and raised in

Washington Heights, he claims to have suffered an awful childhood under the control of a suffocatingly overprotective mother; as a result he was neurotic, fearful, and had a tendency to cry. He and Joel had not actually met at school but at an alumni party. After they became friends, Joel and Ethan asked Barry if he would film the trailer for a fee of $100. Sonnenfeld was not much older than Joel but had already worked on a number of documentaries, including *In Our Water* (released in 1982), which received an Academy Award nomination.

Given his fragile personality, it is surprising that Sonnenfeld would later go on to direct his own films, including the highly successful and stylish *Get Shorty* and *Men in Black*. But the Coens were giving him a chance at a first feature, and he was happy to take it. Although they discussed the look of the film in detail, Ethan joked, "Actually, we just wanted the movie to be in focus."

With input from Sonnenfeld, Joel and Ethan storyboarded the movie in Austin. Storyboards are a kind of visual depiction of the film's scenes, sketches that lay out each shot, showing not only the actors and a rough sense of the setting, but also, even more importantly, the position of the camera. Different directors rely on their storyboards to a different degree; directors who like to improvise on the set and get input from the cast and crew consider them much less important. But directors who have a clear visual sense of their films, and who like to maintain as much control as possible — Alfred Hitchcock is the most famous example — consider detailed storyboarding to be essential. Joel definitely fell into this latter category. The brothers, in fact, always had a surer sense of what their films should look like than what they meant. With script in hand, the brothers storyboarded their film from the opening shot to the last, covering every scene, cut, and fade-in, no matter how trivial. They worked with three local artists in Austin — one who sketched floor plans, another who did the actual storyboard drawing, and a third who provided additional suggestions — although after *Blood Simple* they would rely on just one storyboard artist, someone who was more on their wavelength.

In the end the storyboards were a sort of comic-strip version of the film itself in which virtually all the camera angles, moves, and creative perspectives were captured. In fact, the storyboards reminded them of the movie parodies in comic form that they had read in *Mad* magazine as kids. The immediate purpose of such intricate storyboarding was practical; if the brothers knew exactly what shots they needed in advance, the filming would go much faster. There would be fewer wasted minutes as they changed their minds and camera and lights had to be moved about for a different angle or approach. In filmmaking, time is money: every day of shooting means paying for cast, crew, equipment rental, location fees, catering, insurance, etc. Also, not having actually directed a feature film before, Joel was terrified of screwing up. He needed the storyboards as a kind of security blanket — a road map that would show him the safe way through the journey.

Besides addressing practical considerations, the storyboarding proved to be almost as creative a process as the writing of the script. By working out the film shot by shot, Joel and Ethan directed it in their imaginations. They "saw" the camera inside the car at night, the windshield obscured by rain; or sweeping along Marty's bar; or dissolving from a window at night to the same window in the morning. In a way, half of their directing effort was done during the storyboard stage, a practice they would continue for all their films.

The next step was the all-crucial casting of the film. Because of the pared-down, laconic style of the script, the actors who inhabited the roles would have to fill in the emotional blanks for the audience. The richest role was certainly that of the slimy private investigator, and knowing that they wanted M. Emmet Walsh, the brothers sent him the script.

Born in Ogdensburg, New York, in 1935, Walsh's television work went as far back as 1959. He had been on *Bonanza*, *The Waltons*, *The Rockford Files*, and dozens of others. On the big screen he had appeared in *Alice's Restaurant*, *Little Big Man*, *Serpico*, *Nickelodeon*, *Slap Shot*, and many other films, including playing the role of Earl Frank in *Straight Time*, the film that made the brothers want him for theirs. Like many character actors, his name was unfamiliar to the public but his face stirred feelings of familiarity.

Whatever uneasiness the hard-working actor felt getting a proposal from a couple of nobodies was overcome by the quality of the material. "When I read the script," Walsh remembered, "I said, 'This character is so much fun, I'll flesh him out and use him in an important movie six or seven years down the road.' Because no one was ever going to hear about this movie. At best, it would be third bill at an Alabama drive-in." Walsh agreed to a meeting and the brothers went to Austin, Texas, to see him. To the older actor the Coens looked like a couple of scrawny kids; he assumed they were being financed by rich, indulgent parents. The brothers showed him the two-minute trailer, the storyboards,

The Coens wanted Holly Hunter for the part of Abby, but settled for
Frances McDormand   PHOTOFEST

which laid out the film in exact detail, and the rigorous shooting schedule. "I
realized they knew exactly what they were doing," Walsh explained.

For the other lead male roles, the brothers turned again to experienced but
affordable actors. For Marty, the two-timed husband, they chose Dan Hedaya,
a bushy-eyebrowed, restless-jawed actor with an intense stare. A veteran of such
films as *True Confessions*, *Endangered Species*, and *The Hunger*, he was probably
best known for his continuing role as Macafee in the celebrated television series
Hill Street Blues. Whoever played Ray, the younger lover, would need to be more
appealing if the audience was going to feel sympathetic towards him. The fair-
haired John Getz was attractive but in a mild, real way; he didn't look like a
standard Hollywood hunk. While he had done some feature work (*Thief of
Hearts*), most of his experience was off-Broadway and on television shows such
as *Wonder Woman*, *Barney Miller*, and his own series, *Rafferty*.

The actor that would prove most important, however, was none of these
already-knowns. Instead, it was a young, unknown woman who would come to
play a central role in the career of the Coen brothers — and in their personal
lives as well.

The Preacher's Daughter

Frances McDormand was born in 1958, the daughter of a Disciples of Christ preacher from Canada. The family traveled all through the Bible Belt during Frances's early years, finally settling down in Pennsylvania when she was eight. Although she did not get to go to live theater or cinemas, McDormand developed a passion for acting when she was cast as Lady Macbeth in a high school production.

McDormand studied at the Yale School of Drama and then performed in regional theater productions. With her thin blond hair, slim and uncurvy figure, and prominent mouth, she felt extremely insecure about her looks. At one point early in her career she went to Hollywood to try and break in, going to auditions only to find herself surrounded by beautiful women in short skirts. Discouraged, she stopped trying to compete for glamorous roles; when she did win a part she worked to make herself look less rather than more attractive. The only real professional role she had before *Blood Simple* was a small continuing role on *Hill Street Blues*.

In fact, it wasn't McDormand whom the brothers first wanted for the role of Abby. It was her roommate, another young actress who had been more successful getting film and television parts but who still wasn't very well-known: Holly Hunter. Hunter and McDormand had met at Yale and then roomed together in New York. "Frances always had wonderful instincts," Hunter said of those days. "Even when I first knew her I felt she had a real strong sense of who she is." Hunter auditioned for the brothers first but couldn't do the role because of a schedule conflict, so she encouraged Frances to try out for these "two really weird guys" who were making their first film. McDormand had trouble even getting an audition, but she finally managed to read for them and the brothers liked what they saw. It was only her second professional job but already her first step towards roles not only in other Coen brothers films, but also on Broadway. She would be the first, but not the last important acting discovery that the Coen brothers would make. Hunter, by the way, did manage to sneak into *Blood Simple*. She is the uncredited voice of a woman on Meurice's answering machine.

In New York the department heads were hired; the crew would be picked up in Austin. For the production design they signed on Jane Musky, a Boston University theater graduate who had painted scenery for England's Pinewood

Studios and the English National Opera before coming to New York. She was introduced to the brothers by Mark Silverman, the film's associate producer. Also enlisted was a coach to help the leads, all non-Texans, give the dialogue an authentic Texan twang. The brothers might not have known anything about Texas beyond its myth, but they wanted their characters to talk like real natives.

And so, with cast and crew in place, and temporary quarters set up in Austin, the shooting of *Blood Simple* began.

Here Comes the Shakycam

The locations for shooting had already been scouted out in Austin and nearby Hutto. For Marty's bar, a real bar — the Soap Creek Saloon, where Hank Williams once sang — was chosen. The huge model of a steer outside prefigured the statue of Paul Bunyan that would appear in *Fargo*.

Shooting began on October 4, 1982, and lasted for a mere eight weeks. Joel was 29 years old, Ethan only 26. The last film that they had actually made together was in Super-8, when they were still kids; now they had big 35-mm cameras, trucks of equipment, crew members buzzing all around. It was an enormous responsibility and, frankly, the brothers were scared. But they didn't show it, and they didn't hold back. Instead, feeling that they had little to lose, Ethan and Joel urged each other to just "go for it."

Although the brothers had decided to call Joel the director and Ethan the producer, each would really act as both. It might be fair to say that Joel was the senior director and Ethan the junior, for the older brother did most of the communicating with the actors while Ethan paced in the background, but the two made decisions together, and there never seemed to be a disagreement between them.

Not everyone around them felt as confident as the brothers made themselves appear. Plagued by a bad case of nerves, Sonnenfeld often retched on the set. The young Frances McDormand, acting in a feature for the first time, felt less than confident that the brothers would actually be able to complete the picture. She would later say that her "dumb" look on the screen was a result of her feeling "paralyzed until they told me what to do." Being a veteran, M. Emmet Walsh was perhaps best able to keep cool. But he would tease the brothers by saying,

"Let's cut this sophomoric stuff, it's not NYU anymore." When Joel politely asked the actor to do something just to "humor" him, Walsh replied, "Joel, this whole damn movie is just to humor you."

What probably saved them was the meticulous work they had done on the storyboards, laying out every shot and camera position. Indeed, because everything had been worked out in advance, Sonnenfeld could shoot footage that would allow for sophisticated editing afterwards: match cuts, sound overlaps, dissolves. Joel's plan had been to keep the camera moving, a style that both naturally appealed to him and that he had picked up from Sam Raimi, but because they could not afford cranes and other pricey equipment they had to improvise. And so Sonnenfeld, who operated the camera himself (many Hollywood cinematographers do not), sometimes shot while lying on a blanket that could be dragged along or even lifted into the air. A device they borrowed from Raimi, who had learned it from Caleb Deschanel who had used it on *More American Graffiti*, was called the shakycam. A twelve-foot-long pole with handles at each end and the camera mounted in the middle, the shakycam was carried by two people who would race along with it. Using a wide-angle lens on the camera, the shakycam could move from wide-angle to close-up with dizzying speed.

Even more ingenuity went into another effect late in the film. Abby goes to Marty's office to see what has happened to him; from there she seems to fall into the bed in her apartment. To achieve this startling illusion the brothers strapped McDormand to what Sonnenfeld called "a torture device" that had the camera attached to it. Changing the backdrop while the device made her drop appeared on film as if she were falling through space and time.

While the brothers had considered shooting in black and white for a film-noir look, they decided that the movie would appear too independent, low-budget, and marginal. "We wanted to trick people into thinking we'd made a real movie," Ethan said. But they still decided to keep the film dark and to use color as a source of light when they could. Despite needing to film quickly to keep to their schedule, they managed many shots and sequences that show an extraordinary attention to visual detail. When Abby and Ray have sex in the hotel room, the camera prowls across them and light from passing cars stripes the walls. After Marty is shot by the private investigator, the camera looks down on him slumped in his office chair from *above* the blades of the revolving fan. This shot, however, took longer than expected to set up and Joel almost gave up on it for fear of going over budget. As for the violence, the Coens worked hard to make it feel real. Ethan said, "When you're thinking about how to handle a murder, you can either say, 'This character dies,' or you can make the audience feel it. We want to grab them by the lapels and make them feel it. They're not there to get information; they're there to feel it."

While on some shots there were many crew members buzzing around, at other times it was only Joel, Ethan, and Sonnenfeld with the actors. Shooting the "buried alive" scene, in which Ray covers the still-moving Marty with earth, it was Ethan himself who squirmed beneath the dirt. And while the brothers managed to keep to the budget, setting a standard that they would keep for all of their subsequent films (depending on who you believe is telling the truth about *The Hudsucker Proxy*), by the end of the eight weeks their funds were exhausted. "Even with *Blood Simple*," Ethan said, "where we really did it for a dime, I don't think we ever walked away thinking that whatever mistakes we made or whatever we wished was different would have been different had we twice the budget."

Perhaps not, but just a little extra money would have been nice. When, after wrapping, the brothers decided some reshoots were necessary — a common occurrence in feature-filmmaking — they didn't have the money to hire the actors back. And so they had to use themselves instead. They even had to shoot one scene — of rain coming down hard on a road at night while the camera gives the view from a moving car — back in New York. An old friend, William Preston Robertson, arrived in town with his Honda and they immediately pressed him into service, renting a camera and buying some film. Barry Sonnenfeld rode in the passenger seat operating the camera, mounted with wooden boards and rope on the front bumper (the cable release which allowed him to turn the camera on and off kept malfunctioning), while Joel drove and Ethan and William sat in the back, all of them soaking wet. Somehow they managed to get the shot. Robertson was also pressed into service to provide the voice of the radio evangelist; he is listed in the credits as "Rev. William Preston Robertson."

Oh yes, perhaps it ought to be mentioned that Joel came home with more than footage for a movie. He and Frances McDormand had become a couple during the shoot. McDormand has said, "We were both doing, for the first time, what we wanted to do for the rest of our lives." It was a real love story to complement the more brutal fictional one. McDormand, it turned out, would have to be a patient wife; her husband would not give her another leading part for almost ten years.

Late Nights

It is a sad truth that many low-budget films are begun but never completed, or if completed never find a distributor. Joel and Ethan now had their cans of raw footage; it was time to make them into a finished movie.

Not having any money was definitely a drawback. For one thing, they couldn't hire an experienced editor who could make the best of what they had shot. On the plus side, the brothers wanted to keep a tight control over their own creation, and so what would be the point of letting someone else edit the film? The brothers would do it themselves, using a pseudonym — Roderick Jaynes — so that their own names wouldn't appear too often in the credits, as frequently happened on low-budget films. In fact, they liked their alter ego so much — and they admitted to getting a "juvenile thrill" from performing this little hoax — that they later wrote a scathing preface for the book of the *Barton Fink* and *Miller's Crossing* scripts under his name. And of course there would be the matter of Mr. Jaynes earning an Academy Award nomination, but we will save that for its proper place.

A lack of both funds and experience meant that the editing process was a protracted one, taking them most of 1983. But it was a process that the brothers found themselves liking. "In the postproduction," McDormand said, "that's when they get to lead the artistic life; they get to stay up late and get circles under their eyes and smoke too much and not eat enough and be focused entirely on creating something." If anything, the film became darker and more serious; several short scenes or parts of scenes with more comic intent did not make it into the final cut. One moment — the much-praised tracking shot along the bar, with the camera rising over a sleeping drunk and moving back again — did not make the first edit. When Sonnenfeld asked why, Joel muttered, "I don't know. It just seemed too self-conscious to me." Sonnenfeld replied, "Joel, this whole movie is self-conscious." The shot went in.

The motion picture is a hybrid art form, consisting of visual images, language, and music. Music has always been part of the texture of the film experience, heightening the drama and the emotion, underscoring the experience of the characters, cueing the audience whether to react to what appears on the screen with laughter or sympathy or a racing heart. The score for Sam Raimi's *The Evil Dead* had been of the typical horror-movie kind. Once again aiming higher, the Coens wanted a score both more subtle and more evocative, one that affected the audience's emotions without beating them over the head. Joel and Ethan might have worked up the confidence to write, shoot, and edit their own movie, but even they would have to relinquish some control and allow a composer to contribute to the film. The problem was, of course, that well-known film composers are hugely expensive. Time for the brothers to make another discovery.

Blood Simple's sound editor, Skip Lievsay, had a friend named Carter Burwell. A graduate of Harvard, Burwell worked by day in computer graphics and moonlighted as a keyboard player in different bands. He went to meet the brothers, who screened for him a reel of the film. Burwell went home, wrote some music, and brought it back for the brothers to hear. They liked it but had some trouble convincing the people around them to put their faith in someone who had never scored a feature film before. In the end, of course, the Coen brothers won out. What Burwell came up with was a haunting piano melody, quick-tempoed, rhythmically complex, and full of understated, brooding tension. It was a beautiful complement to the images on the screen.

With the score ready, at last the film was complete. The brothers had written it in 1980, raised the money to make it in 1981, shot it in 1982, and edited it in 1983. The film had come out better than anyone could have expected; to borrow Ethan's word, it actually did look like a "real" film. Now it was 1984 and all they had to do was find a distributor. How hard could that be?

Finding an Audience

Joel and Ethan's first move was to fly to Los Angeles with their cans of film and screen them for the distribution arms of all the major studios. That this turned out to be a humiliating process was no doubt part of what turned them off Hollywood and left them wary of ever compromising their artistic freedom for

Mutual suspicion undermines the romance of Frances McDormand and John Getz in *Blood Simple*   EVERETT COLLECTION

a big studio deal. Sitting in those screening rooms, the brothers had to endure listening to the studio executives' "garbage," as Joel put it. One studio head kept spitting out sunflower shells as he watched; in the middle of the screening he suddenly said aloud, "Why is *Revenge of the Nerds* making so much money?"

Between screenings the frustrated brothers invented increasingly bizarre film scenarios. How about a movie in which Hitler's parents immigrate to the United States and Adolf becomes an agent in Hollywood? By the end of the trip virtually every major distributor had turned *Blood Simple* down. In truth, most of the executives had enough taste to admire the movie; the real problem was that the marketing departments couldn't figure out how to package it. That year several independent films had done well at the box office: Jim Jarmusch's *Stranger Than Paradise*, John Sayles's *Brother From Another Planet*, and Alan Rudolph's *Choose Me*. But all of them were clearly art-house pictures that appealed to a young and sophisticated audience. *Blood Simple* wasn't an art film but a film-noir-style thriller. But audiences expected thrillers to have recognizable stars, more action, a glossier look, and perhaps most important, at least one or two characters to sympathize with. *Blood Simple* had far more of an emotional coolness to it; it didn't quite allow the audience to like anybody.

Most frustrating was that Joel and Ethan believed that, given a chance, audiences would like the film. They had some proof too, in its warm reception at film festivals. Its first public showing was at the USA Film Festival in Dallas, where it won the Grand Jury Prize. (After winning, the brothers received a congratulatory letter from Rudy Perpich, the governor of Minnesota. Joel hung it in his bathroom.) It was well-received by other festival audiences too. Finally it was seen by a man who would prove to be an important figure in the early part of the Coens' career: Ben Barenholtz.

Barenholtz had been bringing movies to audiences for a long time. In 1968, he opened New York's Elgin Cinema, a revival and art-film house, where he originated the "Midnight Movie" showing. He formed Libra Films Corporation in 1975 to distribute independent films, handling Peter Brook's *Meetings With Remarkable Men*, John Sayles's first film, *Return of the Secaucus Seven*, and David Lynch's first, *Eraserhead*. Barenholtz sold Libra, only to start a new company, Circle Releasing, with two brothers, Ted and Jim Pedas, who had also run repertory houses.

Barenholtz liked the film and Ethan and Joel liked him. They also liked his good track record with independent films that had crossed over to a more mainstream audience. "They're sensitive, determined, and know what they want," Barenholtz said of the Coens. "Their objective is to have total artistic freedom. The priority was never the money. It's the work. They want to work without interference. So I created that context." What Barenholtz meant by "context" was a three-picture deal in which Circle Releasing agreed not only to distribute the films in the U.S. but also to leave the brothers alone to make the films they wanted. Circle could not ask the brothers to cast big stars, change the script, or re-edit the films.

Among the other festivals that the brothers took their film to were the Toronto Film Festival, Cannes, and the New York Film Festival. It was at Cannes that some real buzz first began to develop around the film, which was shown out of competition. The brothers had also signed with a company called Skouras Films and it was their job to sell foreign rights to *Blood Simple*. Before long they had made deals with distributors in Great Britain, Australia, South Africa, Belgium, and Luxembourg, with more pending. Meanwhile, the film received a rave review in *Variety*, the powerful industry newspaper. "An inordinately good low-budget film-noir thriller," the paper declared. "Performances are top-notch all around. . . ." At the New York Film Festival the good notices continued. Janet Maslin of the *New York Times* began her review this way: "Black humor, abundant originality and a brilliant visual style make Joel Coen's *Blood Simple* a directorial debut of extraordinary promise." She noted its film-noir origins but also that it was full of "wit." And she made a remark that would apply to several subsequent Coen brothers films as well: "A lot of dying is done in *Blood Simple* and almost none of it is done right."

It was at the festival in New York that the American press got its first real look at this interesting duo. They saw the six-foot-tall Joel with his dark, deep-set eyes and long hair that often fell over his face, his tendency to slouch, his uniform of jeans and T-shirt. And Ethan, three inches shorter than his brother, with finer features, curly hair, and wire-rimmed glasses. Like his brother, he preferred jeans and T-shirts and chain-smoked his Camel Lights. Ethan was the more restless one, with a tendency to giggle and sometimes even bray like a donkey. Reticent by nature, neither Joel nor Ethan enjoyed being the center of attention. During the screening of their film, they both sat in the lobby. At the press conference, reporters were somewhat baffled by this pair of brothers who did not seem to take the occasion seriously. When asked about their artistic approach, Ethan quoted not one of the philosophers he studied at Princeton, but their buddy Sam Raimi: "The innocent must suffer, the guilty must be punished, you must drink blood to be a man." Did they really see everything as just a joke, or was this some weird form of defensive behavior?

Now with an American distributor and good advance word, *Blood Simple* was finally on the verge of being released. The film that the brothers had begun to write in 1980 opened in selected American theaters in January, 1985. Pushing themselves to be cooperative and hungry to see what the press would make of their film, they dutifully appeared for more interviews. Stephen Schiff of *Vanity Fair* compared them to "a droll heartland comedy team, bouncing wisecracks off each other with the deadpan aplomb that makes one a smash on the college circuit." They were even interviewed by Jane Pauley on the *Today* show.

And then the reviews came in as critics across the country rushed either to praise the newest cinema geniuses or to expose them as the latest frauds. Most of them came down on the side of the former. The hard-to-please David

Denby of *New York* magazine called *Blood Simple* "one of the most brazenly self-assured directorial debuts in American film history." To him it was "a hair-raising and funny new gothic thriller . . . driven by lust, jealousy, and greed — the immemorial trinity of pulp fiction." Unlike other recent attempts to revive the film-noir genre, this one had "the soul of the real thing."

David Ansen of *Newsweek* was equally impressed; ". . . a maliciously entertaining murder story," he called it, "at once a bated-breath thriller and a comedy as black as they come." *Vanity Fair*'s Stephen Schiff wrote: "I'll be astonished if the studios give us as brilliant a chiller all year." And Richard Corliss compared Joel in *Time* to one of the greatest American directors when he called *Blood Simple* "a debut film as scarifyingly assured as any since Orson Welles was just this wide."

The film received even more critical attention when it appeared on several top-ten lists of the best films of 1985. *Time*, the *Washington Post*, and USA *Today* all put it on their lists. Because it was the visual style and the confidence of the direction that the critics noticed most, director Joel received the most attention and praise. Of course the critics did not know that Ethan had a hand in the direction too, and Ethan certainly gave no sign of feeling any envy. After all, if it weren't for Joel's prodding, Ethan wouldn't have helped make a film at all. But it is interesting to wonder whether the younger brother would sometimes feel a need to define himself in a way that did not depend on his brother or result in his brother's shadow being cast over his own. Perhaps some of this understandable resentment was behind the collection of short stories he later wrote and published — with his name alone attached.

Like almost all subsequent Coen brothers films, *Blood Simple* also had its detractors — critics who seemed to take personal exception to the good reviews the film had received and wanted to shout that the emperor had no clothes. As Sheila Benson put it in the *Los Angeles Times*, the Coens "are long on slick glossy style, no dispute, and they have a nice way with actors. But in this case, style is the sleight-of-hand used to divert us from the thinness of the plot. . . . What no one writing about the film seems to have felt is the deep unpleasantness of this exercise in empty style. . . ." J. Hoberman in the *Village Voice* could not help admiring the humor and style, but he also found the film "callous" and "thin." And he ended his review with a phrase that Ethan would later quote with apparent relish: "Beneath the tinsel, this film has the heart of a Bloomingdale's window and the soul of a résumé." In fact, the *Village Voice*, arguably the brothers' hometown paper since it is published in New York where they live, would prove itself over time to be more skeptical of the brothers' talents than just about any other publication. The *Voice*'s writers would have some especially strong opinions on the Coens' depiction of Jews and gays.

One might have expected the grand duchess of American Film criticism, Pauline Kael of the *New Yorker*, to feel some sympathy for these young filmmakers with their strong visual style. But Kael condemned the film as "a splatter-movie art movie," calling it a student film on a larger scale. She also blasted those critics who fell for its sizzle, insisting that Joel Coen's camera flourishes were noteworthy only because the film had nothing to say.

And so the debate over the Coens was established early; they were brilliant and innovative stylists, but was style enough? Did their films lack "heart and soul" or did those who think so merely prefer conventional films with characters they could like and stories that had emotionally comforting endings? These were questions that would become more complex as the Coens made more — and more ambitious — films. For now it might do to remember Joel's remark that *Blood Simple* was a "phony film," an exercise in filmmaking and a homage to the film-noir genre rather than anything really new. If not a great film, or even a brilliant one (despite its brilliant visual moments), it was nevertheless a remarkable debut, and, for those who were willing to accept its self-imposed limitations, an entertaining film as well.

Blood Simple was not a big hit, but it was a success. The film made $3 million, peanuts for a major Hollywood production but respectable for an independent film, and more than enough to turn a profit, given *Blood Simple*'s modest budget. The urban audience came, if in small numbers. While critics were divided, the public tended to side with those who felt the film lacked warmth. As one journalist wrote, "the public found it slow and cold and filled with hateful characters." Well, not all the public. It isn't hard to find fans of *Blood Simple* among avid moviegoers.

And it was certainly successful enough — and controversial enough — to make Joel and Ethan known to the public. On the eve of its opening in New York, the *Times* ran a profile of them (in which the brothers declared that they planned to collaborate for the rest of their careers). Other publications began to follow suit. Hollywood producers started calling to take them out to dinner, often giving them books to read — "properties" that the producers owned and wanted adapted for the screen. On one of these occasions Ethan ordered his first-ever steak tartare — medium-rare. The studio bigshots pretended not to notice. Steven Spielberg invited them to visit. Even Hugh Hefner asked them to drop in at the Playboy mansion — an invitation that may have inspired the character of Jackie Treehorn in *The Big Lebowski*, who is in part based on Hefner.

While they enjoyed the success of the film, Joel and Ethan were wary enough of the attention not to let it go to their heads. Joel suggested that all the press interviews and articles were the result of reporters beginning to get sick of writing about *Beverly Hills Cop*. "The press was tired of writing about it and was hungry for something else. It looks like we're it. Now they're reviewing each other's reviews. Let's face it: it's only a movie." In any case, neither Joel nor Ethan was interested in changing his life or going to Hollywood parties. They weren't looking for studio deals or multi-million dollar contracts. But they didn't want to become the darlings of the indie-film set either. Instead, they preferred hanging out with old friends like Sam Raimi. The people at Circle Releasing even assumed that the Coens would want to be released from their contract to move on to a major studio, but they were wrong. What Ethan and Joel wanted was to make another movie. *Their* movie, *their* way.

CHAPTER THREE

TRIAL RUN

CRIMEWAVE

"If it's so funny, why don't you share it with the rest of us?"
— Crazed driver in *Crimewave*

Before Joel and Ethan made their next movie, though, they would receive another lesson in the dangers of studio film-making — or, rather, signing a contract that gives power over your film to somebody else. In this case it was *The XYZ Murders*, the script that the Coens wrote with Sam Raimi before writing their own *Blood Simple*. Intended as a parody of thrillers — unlike the Coens' own films, which often play off genres but never take the easy route of flat-out parody — the script opens with a carful of nuns driving to the Hudsucker State Penitentiary. (The name "Hudsucker" would, of course, recur in another Coen brothers–Raimi script.) At the prison is a condemned man named Vic, sitting on death row for murdering the owner of the security company where he worked. About to be executed, Vic recounts the circumstances that have led to this tragic moment, beginning with one partner in the security firm hiring a pair of rat exterminators to kill the other partner.

Reed Birney and Sheree J. Wilson in *Crimewave,* a cartoon version of things to come   EVERETT COLLECTION

Set in Detroit, primarily because it was Sam Raimi's hometown, the story involves plenty of action, chase scenes, and a few dead bodies.

Ethan and Joel would receive billing credit for the screenplay above Raimi, indicating that they were more responsible for it. Some of its slapstick humor, worthy of the Three Stooges (jabs in the face, a steel plate in someone's head), seems more in Raimi's style. In any case, the script shows more sophomoric energy and enthusiasm than skill and makes interesting viewing for aficionados of the Coen brothers primarily for the many scenes and images that foreshadow the later films. When the partner hires the exterminators, for instance, he pre-figures Marty hiring the private investigator to kill his wife and her lover in *Blood Simple.* And when one of the exterminators tries to kill the partner's wife, his attempts to get at her — including the breaking of a light and crashing his hand through a door — is nothing more than a crude trial run for *Blood Simple*'s climax. When the exterminator finally captures her and ties her up, she tries to hop away — just like Jerry Lundegaard's wife in *Fargo.* Indeed, the comic-sadistic exterminators are cartoon versions of *Fargo*'s hired kidnappers, Carl Showalter and Gaear Grimsrud, and the film's basic comic narrative (hired killers who get out of control) contains the seed of *Fargo*'s more realistic one (hired kidnappers who get out of control).

The long comic chase scene in *The XYZ Murders* shows the origins of the action sequence in *Raising Arizona*, and there's a jitterbug dance scene that is very similar to the USO dance in *Barton Fink*. And when the hapless hero Vic hangs desperately off a bridge, afraid of plunging to his doom, he seems to be an early version of Norville Barnes, who ends up hanging out the window of the Hudsucker building. In fact, the storytelling strategy of *The XYZ Murders* — a man who may be about to die has his story told in flashback before he is rescued at the last moment — will be duplicated, somewhat more artfully, in *The Hudsucker Proxy*.

The film also appears to have influenced Barry Sonnenfeld, who didn't even work on it. Years later, when he directed *Men in Black*, he would have the evil alien drive around in an exterminator's truck that looked a lot like the one in *The XYZ Murders* — with a giant model rat on its roof.

While the brothers co-wrote the screenplay for *The XYZ Murders* with their friend, it belonged to Raimi, who hoped to produce it through his and Robert Tapert's own company, Renaissance Pictures, along with another producer, if they could find someone willing to put up the money. Raimi and Tapert and their friend, Bruce Campbell from *The Evil Dead*, approached an independent producer named Edward R. Pressman. Known for supporting young talent, Pressman had been involved in producing *Badlands*, *Conan the Barbarian*, and the international German success, *Das Boot*. The three friends had first met him at the Sitges film festival where they had gone to promote *The Evil Dead*. (If there's one thing that Sam Raimi's career proves, it's the old advice that to get into the film business you have to schmooze, schmooze, schmooze.)

Pressman liked the script and took it to Embassy Pictures. The studio agreed to distribute the film and help finance it, in return for final cut of the picture. While it is not only common practice but the usual rule for studios to demand final cut, independent filmmakers usually consider this an unacceptable interference in their creative control. But it is the necessary price to pay for signing with a big — or in this case medium-sized — studio, and Raimi decided to bite the bullet. Casting the film, he hired a New York theater actor named Reed Birney to play Vic, Louise Lasser, the only "name" in the cast, as the annoying wife; he also gave parts to Bruce Campbell and Frances McDormand (as a nun).

Even the producer, Edward R. Pressman, got a role. Shooting took place in Detroit in early winter. The weather turned much colder than expected and the cameras had to be wrapped in heating pads. But Embassy turned out to be less than thrilled with the finished film; they took it away from Raimi and had it re-edited, changing its name, first to — believe it or not — *Broken Hearts and Noses*, then to *Crimewave*.

Raimi, as well as Joel and Ethan (perhaps in support of their friend) denounced Embassy's recut, claiming that the studio ruined the picture in the editing room. It seems likely, however, that no matter who did the editing, *Crimewave* was not going to turn out to be a great film. As in *The Evil Dead*, the acting is amateurish, while Raimi's direction is heavy-handed, ridiculously exaggerating the jokes. On the other hand, the busy camera work is amusing and the special effects — from an electrical pole toppling onto a car to the mad chase where the characters standing on the roofs have to duck so as not to be brained by overhead bridges — do keep it visually compelling. Perhaps if Raimi had been able to retain control it wouldn't have seemed as "unfocussed" as Vincent Canby called it in his *New York Times* review after the film's very limited release — in New York it only played the Thaliain — in May 1985, just four months after *Blood Simple*. Canby called the film "a comedy made by and for movie buffs — people whose view of the world has been shaped almost exclusively by movies rather than first-hand experience." While Canby found the picture tough to sit through and overly cartoonish (a description that would apply more positively to the Coens' second film), he did note that it was "amazingly elaborate for a low-budget movie." Raimi, like the Coens, knew how to get the most for his money.

Perhaps what is most interesting is that the reviewers' criticisms of *Crimewave* sound like the later praise for the Coen brothers' own films, but turned upside down. Rick Groen of the Toronto *Globe and Mail* wrote, "Watching [*Crimewave*] is a bit like reading a derivative essay from a bright but lazy student — the quotes come thick and fast, yet there's nothing original in between." Groen also complained that the film awkwardly mixed two genres, screwball comedy and film noir. Those critics who liked the Coens' own pictures would later applaud these very traits — the clever film references and the unusual mixture of genres.

But *Crimewave* also got some better reviews, if not raves. *Variety* called it a "boisterous, goofy, cartoonish comedy in the *Airplane* mold . . . a passably funny entertainment." And the *Village Voice* found similar things to like: "Imagine a Jerry Lewis extravaganza about serial killers, with a style out of comic books and Warner cartoons. . . ."

Maybe it was a question of whether or not you liked cartoons. Not that it mattered; *Crimewave* turned out to be a mere blip on a filmgoer's radar screen, here and gone, leaving hardly a trace. For Ethan and Joel it had turned out to be a warm-up writing exercise and an interesting example of the dangerous power of studios.

CHAPTER FOUR

BABY WRANGLING

RAISING ARIZONA

"These were the salad days."
— H.I. McDonnough in *Raising Arizona*

Joel and Frances McDormand, a committed couple after the filming of *Blood Simple*, moved in together. And it was around the time of the Coens' second film that Ethan endured his first, short-lived marriage to a woman named Hilary. Both Ethan and Joel have been admirably tight-lipped about discussing their private lives in the media, and so little is known of the marriage — other than the fact that the two slipped away to get married at city hall just before shooting of the new film began — including how long it even lasted. It does seem curious, however, that Ethan, who followed his brother to New York, and into the film business, also followed his matrimonial pattern: a brief, failed relationship followed by a long-term, successful one.

No longer living together, the brothers took an office on West 23rd Street in an industrial building otherwise occupied by printing and graphics businesses. In May 1985, in their one room with dirty windows, the brothers began their scriptwriting process. They were still living hand-to-mouth, eating donuts while they wrote, making coffee in a tin pan on the stove.

They moped. They smoked. Joel lay on the sofa. Ethan paced.

The one thing they knew was that they wanted to make a film as different from *Blood Simple* as possible. "We didn't want to do another scary movie," Ethan said. "We'd already gotten that out of our system. Also, *Blood Simple* was slow and deliberate. We wanted to try something with a faster pace and a lighter tone."

They came up with the story of H.I. (or Hi) McDonnough, a repeatedly incarcerated robber of convenience stores who falls in love with a prison guard named Edwina. Once out of jail, he and Edwina marry and move into a trailer home, and Hi tries to go straight. But when the couple fail to conceive a child, Hi finds no solution to Edwina's suffering but to kidnap one of the "Arizona Quintuplets," the five children born, with the help of fertility drugs, to Mrs. and Mr. Nathan Arizona, the unpainted-furniture king. Hi's recidivist tendencies are encouraged by the appearance of two brothers, old prison buddies on the lam who take up unwanted residence in their home and who decide to kidnap the baby back in order to collect the reward money. Matters are made more complicated and ominous by a bounty-hunting biker who seems like the incarnation of hell itself as he rises out of Hi's nightmares into real life. The brothers imagined it full of comic speeches and wild chase scenes in which they would take their inspiration from Chuck Jones's *Roadrunner* cartoons. Perhaps the location — Arizona — even owes something to the desert landscapes through which Wile E. Coyote eternally chased that beep-beeping bird.

If anything, the brothers were moving even farther from any autobiographical roots. Their characters were not university-educated Jews, but, to use a pejorative term, "trailer trash." Neither Joel nor Ethan had any experience with babies. Still, writing a movie about a woman wanting a child didn't seem odd to them. "We're not really intimately acquainted with murder either," Joel said, "and we made a movie about killing people." Ethan did feel that somewhere there was a "personal connection" to the story but he couldn't identify it. He also said, "It strikes me that what we're really most attracted to is something which is totally foreign to our experience."

Later, some critics noticed that a number of filmmakers were suddenly finding the American heartland to be exotic territory worthy of exploration, rather

Foreign to their experience; Joel and Ethan Coen on the set of *Raising
Arizona*   PHOTOFEST

than either the East or the West Coasts, which are the settings for most movies. *Blue Velvet* was the most striking example, but there were others. While the Coens acknowledged the trend by calling it "the Hayseed Renaissance," they immediately claimed to have little interest in it. But then, throughout their careers, the Coens have not liked to be identified with any other group of filmmakers.

Like *Blood Simple*, *Raising Arizona* seems to have something to say about the nature of American life: Americans are a romantic people who believe in the possibilities of love, of wanting and expecting happiness, and of redemption. They are a people at once childish and adult, shallow and deep. Did Joel and Ethan really intend to make such statements? Quite possibly. In fact, the brothers, who had already rewritten James M. Cain for their first film, may well have drawn on a classic American novel as the inspiration for *Raising Arizona*. An academic critic named Rodney Hill contends that the film is based on John Steinbeck's famous novel *Of Mice and Men*. And while the two stories are hardly parallel, Hill makes a good case for it, showing how the brothers borrowed "Steinbeck's theme of small Americans and their misguided dreams." The brothers themselves seem to have planted a small clue: the biker from hell is named Leonard Smalls, an odd detail considering that the biker needs no name at all. In *Of Mice and Men* the big, mentally slow man is named Lennie Small.

It's quite possible that the brothers — or more precisely Ethan, the one with the literary bent — used Steinbeck as a source of language too. After all, in their St. Louis Park neighborhood there weren't too many people who said "ain't" for "isn't" and "more'n" for "more than." And there's another possible literary source: the great southern novels of William Faulkner. Faulkner's series about the Snopes family, with their countrified, poetic language and their grotesque actions may have generally influenced the screenplay. Here Ethan and Joel threw in another clue: the brothers who break out of prison are none other than Gale and Evelle Snopes.

But the Coens would always be influenced by an unruly mix of sources, high and low, literary and popular; it is one of their defining traits. The Snopes boys were imagined from the start as a kind of Laurel and Hardy duo, with Gale as the bigger one and Evelle as the Stan Laurel type — although the roles reversed on casting. As for film influences, screwball comedies were a general source. One critic noted that the film resembled *Bringing Up Baby* with a real baby in place of the leopard. The Coens also drew on *Bonnie and Clyde*, Fellini's *Roma* (they liked the use of voice-over at the end), and *The Road Warrior*, out of which their biker from hell seems to have roared.

And so Joel and Ethan began to write, with Ethan at the Smith-Corona electric typewriter. "We never preplan," Joel explained after the film was released. "We don't know what's going to happen next, let alone at the end. And when the process starts to get boring, we know it's time to move in another direction." As for the tag-team process, Ethan said, "We're always in sync about what the film is about. It doesn't mean we don't disagree, because the idea is not to compromise one's point of view. There's no benefit to the film if you defer, so we fight with one another when we feel something is integral to the story." For example, early in the script the brothers were at a loss as to what direction to take the story. Ethan made a suggestion, Joel didn't take to it, and Ethan made another. "You mean make him sort of a retard?" Joel asked of the character they were discussing. When Ethan replied in the affirmative, Joel said, "To me that just wastes time."

Nor did they do any research — about the setting of Arizona, or prison, or even taking care of babies for that matter. The script that came out is miles away from *Blood Simple*, its down-home characters not closed-mouthed but ready to offer speeches, jokes, homilies, and observations on the meaning and strangeness of life. Hi's voice-overs do not come out loud or showy, but almost deadpan, with a formal, rhetorical grace to them — a kind of hick eloquence that would be one of the brother's trademarks. As for the story, it moves as fast as a rollercoaster, from the long opening prologue sequence setting up the marriage of Hi and Ed, which the brothers tried to give a "once upon a time" feel, as if it were the beginning of a fairy tale, to the eerily sentimental finale. The characters are big, even over the top — they don't just speak, they weep and bellow out their emotions.

While the character who provides the engine for the plot is Edwina and her need for a baby, it is Hi who is really the film's center. "He is a thinker," Ethan said of him. "He struggles with the grand issues. He just has an irrepressible urge to hold up convenience stores." Joel added, "The character is caught in an internal struggle. He's being torn in two directions. On the one side is his desire to settle down and have a family. On the other side is his inclination to respond to the call of the wild."

The brothers had a lot of fun writing the other characters as well: Nathan

Arizona, the king of unpainted furniture who, even in his grief at the kidnapping of his son, cannot help making a pitch for his store to the gathered media; Hi's boss, Glen, with his Polock jokes and his nudge-nudge suggestion of wife-swapping to cure Hi's malaise; and the Snopes brothers, dumb Evelle and smooth-talking Gale, the precursor of *Barton Fink*'s Charlie Meadows. Not a minor character goes by that the brothers don't give some peculiar thing to say or do. It was as if, after the repressed, laconic style of *Blood Simple*, the brothers couldn't hold anything back.

While the success of the film had a lot to do with the humor, it is the screenplay's warmth or heart — the very thing that some critics felt was lacking in *Blood Simple* — that makes it so appealing. In Edwina's hunger for a baby of her own, the brothers touch on a near-universal emotion. And while Nathan Jr. is deliberately treated in a cartoon-like manner — like being left in the middle of the highway with cars zipping past — audiences would still find it easy to respond to the smiling, bright-eyed baby. And by making everyone in the film, including the Snopes brothers, susceptible to Nathan Jr.'s charms, the Coens present a reassuring world to the audience in which they can be confident that nothing bad will really happen to the baby.

The question is: where did this "heart" come from? Were these the same filmmakers who reveled in a villain trying to remove a knife pinning down his own hand? Ethan and Joel would claim that they had no emotional attachment to the baby theme; it was simply a device to make the film work. If anything, they seemed to enjoy denying it. In one interview Joel said, "You have a scene in a movie when someone gets shot, right? Bang! And the squib [a special effect simulating a bullet striking] goes off and the blood runs down and you get a reaction, right? It's movie fodder, you know what I mean? And in a really different way, a baby's face is movie fodder. You just wanna take elements that are good fodder and do something different with them." It is interesting to note that after *Raising Arizona* the brothers did not have a really popular film again until they created a character who was pregnant.

Casting Call

The script did not take long to write and when it was done Joel and Ethan handed it over to Circle Releasing for approval. Previously the company had only distributed the brothers' film; this time they were producing it. But this moment was the company's only real involvement in the creative process; they could accept the script and the budget, or turn it down. Ben Barenholtz said afterwards, "What director do you know who had final cut and total artistic control of his second picture? Well, that's what Joel had." He and his partners, the Pedas brothers, liked what they read. Immediately they wrote out a check to Joel and Ethan; Ethan used some of his money to move into a larger apartment downtown with Hilary. On the wall of his old place was the fake hand used in the stabbing scene of *Blood Simple.* Hilary quietly removed it from the decor. The brothers also moved their office to a space in Chelsea, just above Greenwich Village.

Circle was willing to put up half the budget for the film, $3 million. (While still small, the $6-million price tag was about seven times that of *Blood Simple.*) They needed another studio to come in for the rest and took the project to Twentieth Century Fox three weeks into production. Fox agreed to put up the other $3 million and to have no control over the finished film. It was a highly unusual arrangement, but Circle and the brothers insisted on it. Scott Rudin, an executive vice-president at Fox, did not even see his first set of dailies (the raw film footage shot on a particular day) until shooting was almost over.

By August of 1985 the film went into preproduction. Praised for his work on *Blood Simple,* Barry Sonnenfeld, who had just shot another feature, *Compromising Positions,* and won an Emmy Award for his work on a television production called *Out of Step,* signed on again as cinematographer. In December the brothers, along with Sonnenfeld, got together with the storyboard artist. None of them had been happy with the artists who had done the storyboards for their first film, but they found themselves much more pleased with the new one, J. Todd Anderson. Later Ethan would say that Anderson's storyboards reminded him of the Mort Drucker cartoons in *Mad* magazine, which was higher praise from Ethan than if he had compared them to Leonardo da Vinci. The brothers already knew 90 percent of the shots they wanted — "We wouldn't have written the scenes if we didn't know how we were going to shoot them," Joel said. Nevertheless, each scene was drawn using as background the actual locations. Joel also said, "If we didn't preplan it, I don't think we'd be able to handle the pressure. I couldn't walk out there without knowing just what I was after. I'd flounder, and the movie would get away from me, and I'd face the horror of

Nathan Junior, here with Holly Hunter and Nicolas Cage, is a natural
audience heartwarmer in *Raising Arizona*   PHOTOFEST

watching it veer off into the ditch. There's no way to stop it at that point — it's
impossible to wrestle it back on course. It's got its own . . . horrible momentum."

With a larger budget, the brothers could afford to cast a few better-known
actors. Nicolas Cage had just made the not-yet-released Francis Ford Coppola
film, *Peggy Sue Got Married*; his extreme and goofy performance in it so upset
costar Kathleen Turner that she had wanted him fired from the picture. But
Coppola, who happened to be Cage's uncle, refused. In fact, Cage, who dropped
out of high school, made his debut performance in Coppola's *Rumble Fish*.
Since then he had made a reputation as an actor who worked hard on his performances, trying to hit what one director called "complicated notes" with each
performance. By the time the Coen brothers cast him he was only 22, but
already a well-known actor. While he had never actually done a straight-out
comedy before, the conflicted character of Hi seemed just right for him. The
brothers saw casting him as putting "a leading man in a character actor's role."
Cage himself was impressed by the script. "I was sold as soon as I read it. I was
impressed with it because it required no adjustments. It was terrific to finally

find one like that." As for Hi, he said, "What I like best about this character is his humility. He's a very unusual guy. He plays by his own rules, but he's got a lot of integrity." Cage could bring vulnerability and tenderness to the role, qualities that tended to be absent from a Coen brothers script until added by the actors.

If anything, Holly Hunter was even easier to cast. The brothers, who had met her while she was performing in the off-Broadway play *Crimes of the Heart*, had originally wanted her for the lead of *Blood Simple*. In fact, while they didn't exactly write the character of Edwina for her, they did find themselves hearing her voice as they wrote. In the end, they created a part that, as Ethan said, "wasn't a reflection of who Holly is so much as a part it'd be fun to see her play."

Not surprisingly, Hunter too loved the script and jumped at the chance for her first leading feature-film role. "She comes from a long line of police officers and takes pride in the militaristic discipline that cops have," she would say of her character. "In that way, it makes perfect sense that she'd fall in love with Hi because, even though he's an ex-con, he doesn't play games. . . . She also has an incredible maternal instinct — a desperate, abnormal, compulsive desire to have a child. It's bigger than anything she's confronted in her life."

Having grown up in Conyers, Georgia, Hunter began acting in high school, moving to New York after college drama. A diminutive five-foot-two, she nevertheless had a fiery energy that brought life to the parts she played. She was known in the New York theater world for her work in the plays of Beth Henley, and she had appeared in some TV movies and a few films such as the forgettable *Swing Shift*. But it was the Coen brothers who gave Hunter her first chance to really shine on the big screen.

In the long run, though, it was the casting of John Goodman in the role of Gale Snopes that would matter most for the career of the Coen brothers, because it was Goodman who would join the company of recurring actors in their films. And the brothers would write some of their most memorable roles for him. Goodman was a fascinating person, a very self-deprecating actor who undervalued his own talents and was painfully self-conscious of his large size — he is six-foot-three and weighs nearly 300 pounds. Born in St. Louis, he lost his father when he was only two and his mother then had to go to work in a drugstore. Goodman began as a football player in college before switching to acting. In 1975, he moved to New York, where he barely survived on dinner-theater and off-off-Broadway parts. Then came small film roles and a juicier part in the

Broadway musical *Big River*. More films followed, but it was his starring role as Roseanne Barr's husband in the hit TV show *Roseanne* that made him both rich and famous, if no more emotionally secure. Critics often praised his big grace and his charming yet devilish smile. A writer for the *New York Times Magazine* captured some of the qualities that must have attracted Joel and Ethan to him: Goodman, the reporter wrote, was "natural and self-consciously sophisticated, goofy and droll, highbrow and lowbrow, mainstream and eccentric." That description might have just as well have been written about the script of *Raising Arizona*. It was the kind of part that Goodman liked to play, and would in fact play in later Coen brothers films: "They are all men of deep feeling, guys who could explode or start weeping at any moment."

William Forsythe was the first actor who came in to read for the part of Gale. But Forsythe thought the Evelle role was a better fit, so the brothers let him read that one instead. Since Goodman was the next actor coming in, they asked Forsythe if he would stick around so that the two could read together. Ethan said, "They both had these baby faces — they looked like grown-up babies. We just decided on the spot to continue with the baby theme."

Trey Wilson, the man who would play Nathan Arizona, was a veteran Broadway actor who had recently appeared in the films *A Soldier's Story* and *F/X*. The role of the biker went to Randall "Tex" Cobb, a former professional boxer who had given up the gloves for the more genteel trade of acting.

Casting the adults was a piece of cake next to finding the babies to play the Arizona quintuplets. When they set out to write the script, Joel and Ethan had decided to replace the budget-imposed limitations of *Blood Simple* with as many shooting challenges as they could make for themselves. Well, directing babies was certainly one of them. They held an open casting call in Scottsdale, the city they chose as headquarters so there would be a large enough pool of infants, and 400 babies were brought in, all under the age of one. Two casting agents specializing in children, Joseph Schneider and Yvonne Van Orden, were called on to choose 15 babies (three groups of five to be used at a time) to play in the long scene where Hi picks up one and then another from the crib, trying to decide which one to take. The primary talent required: no crying when Mommy goes away. As for Nathan Jr., the plan was to find a pair of twins to make the filming easier. But when the casting agents caught sight of eight-month-old T.J. Kuhn they knew they had found Nathan Jr. The child of a detention officer and a nursing assistant, T.J. was both charming and amazingly even-tempered.

Meanwhile, preproduction work continued. Jane Musky, production designer for *Blood Simple*, was hired on again, and she in turn introduced the brothers to costume designer Richard Hornung, with whom she had worked on the Broadway musical *The News*. Peter Chesney and his company, Image Engineering, came on as the special-effects coordinator. It would be his job to figure out how the biker could pull out his long-barreled gun and shoot a lizard off a rock (the lizard would wear a small harness and be yanked away before the explosion). Barry Sonnenfeld shot some sample scenes on video to make sure that the camera movements the brothers wanted were feasible. Taping at one chosen location, a park with a fountain said to be the world's tallest, he discovered that the glare from the water made the scene impossible to shoot. He worked at getting a "sharp and crisp" look to the film. And once the actors were cast and assembled, the brothers took them through a longer than usual rehearsal period. Joel and Ethan and Barry were worried that shooting a much more complicated film, with chase scenes, more locations, and actors, dogs, and babies could easily run into snags and go into overtime, blowing the schedule and the budget. "There's no question we're more scared," Sonnenfeld admitted.

Babies, Babies Everywhere

The shoot was scheduled for 13 weeks, with a non-union crew to keep costs down. With their tight budget, they could not afford to shoot a lot of film that wouldn't be used. Still, the brothers wanted to have some options in the editing room, so they decided to try to shoot quickly, set up another angle they might want to try, and shoot again. For example, they tried having Nicolas Cage run through the house, holding a camera towards himself to shoot his face close up, but the effect was just too weird.

As before, Joel was the prominent brother on the set while Ethan hung back and smoked, sometimes whispering a suggestion in Joel's ear. Sometimes Ethan did offer editorial direction, but always in complete sync with his brother. For the actors there was one moment that seemed to capture the Coens' uncannily close relationship. "Hey, Joe," Ethan said to his brother. Joel replied, "Yeah, Eth, I know," and then proceeded to tell Nicolas Cage what they both understood without having to say it aloud. Despite their fears, on the set they seemed calm to most of the actors. They were always aware of one another's presence, circling about and meeting to share words; to the cast it was as if they could read each other's mind. They also noted that Joel and Ethan did not talk in artistic terms but simply used film and television references to cue each other: let's have a *Mean Streets* look or a *Love Boat* look, they would say. At one point Joel told Nicolas Cage to give a bit of "Charles Nelson Reilly" in the scene, and Cage knew just what he wanted. Yet to others their anxiety was palpable. Joel developed migraine headaches; he calmed himself down by playing with a Yo-yo.

This wasn't to say that all the actors were always happy on the set. In fact, Joel's reputation for *not* being an actor's director started with *Raising Arizona*. Because the brothers stuck so closely to the storyboards, M. Emmet Walsh, who had a funny cameo as a machine-shop earbender (to use his title in the credits), found there was no room for his suggestions. But the most unhappy was the temperamental Cage, an actor who liked to talk about his "gift" as "something sacred." He had many ideas — for example, he wanted to glance at his watch during a lull in the supermarket chase scene — that were quietly nullified by Joel and Ethan. The script, which had sold him on doing the movie, now seemed to him something like a straitjacket. "Joel and Ethan have a very strong vision," he said during shooting, "and I've learned how difficult it is for them to accept another's artistic vision. They have an autocratic nature." But Cage, who was years younger than them, attributed this uptightness to their youth and thought that with time they would learn to respect "an actor's creative flow." Even Frances McDormand said out loud that she doubted Joel could direct a character-driven film like *Sophie's Choice*.

On the other hand, there was Randall "Tex" Cobb, who told Joel: "You're working with a professional athlete. Try to keep your instructions simple." The reason Cobb's scenes — shot by Sonnenfeld in a deliberately overlit manner to make them more cartoonish — took longer than expected to shoot had nothing to do with angst over the character. It was because Cobb, a lousy motorcyclist, kept missing his mark or stalling the bike.

To be fair to Joel, however, the actors could have some input, especially when it didn't hold up shooting. During a scene in which the Snopes brothers ate up all of Hi and Ed's food while discussing a bank robbery, John Goodman picked up a drumstick and used it to scratch behind his ear. Less acceptable were the

A couple of grown-up babies: John Goodman and Bill Forsythe in
Raising Arizona   20TH CENTURY FOX/SHOOTING STAR

improvisations by the babies. "A baby is somewhere between an actor and a prop," Joel said. "You can't talk to it and tell it what you want to do. And you can't just put it someplace in a shot and reliably predict it'll stay there." Another problem was that babies develop quickly; midway through shooting one baby learned to walk. The brothers fired him.

For the most part, Sonnenfeld, in keeping with Joel's wishes, used wide-angle lenses. A wide-angle lens keeps more of the image in focus so that the audience is not "told" what to look at but can see almost everything equally clearly on the screen. This makes the film look busier and wider, and the backgrounds are more important; the camera itself becomes a more prominent character. It also has the effect of making scenes less intimate, but that too may be an effect the brothers like.

The film's pretitle sequence included a shot of the sun setting over the desert. It took forty minutes to shoot, with motionless stand-ins for Hi and Ed and the camera clicking a frame every three seconds. Later in the film there's a shot of a beautiful sunrise; actually, it was another sunset shot with the camera upside down, the negative reversed afterwards. Two other shots were also done in reverse; one was a trademark Coen dream sequence with the camera racing up a ladder into Nathan Arizona's house, through a window, and into Mrs. Arizona's screaming mouth. Fiber-optic lights around the camera's lens illuminated the actor Lynne Dumin Kitei's tonsils before pulling away. The other had Gale and Evelle Snopes, realizing Nathan Jr. had been left behind, racing back in their car and stopping inches away from him. Of course they couldn't really drive so close and fast to the baby, so they simply started with the car near him and had the driver move backwards, reversing the shot for the film.

During the baby-kidnapping scene Sonnenfeld had to shoot low to the ground. More complicated than just lowering the camera, it required a special mount on a tripod and the use of a prism in front of the lens. Next in difficulty was the chase scene in which Hi, fired from his job, impulsively decides to rob a convenience store while Ed and Nathan Jr. are waiting in the car for him to buy Huggies. It was complicated enough to eat up a good part of the shooting schedule. To follow Hi as he ran, the brothers once again employed the "shaky-cam" instead of a steadycam, this time because it gave a more realistic sense of the character's experience. For other shots, too, they had the grips and gaffers loosen mounts to allow the camera to vibrate energetically — this jittery look made the producers, when they saw the dailies, feel rather jittery themselves.

The scene in which the Snopes brothers burst through the muddy earth in a rainstorm, having escaped from prison, was not easy to shoot either. The prison front was actually the Scottsdale Waterworks. A hole six feet deep was dug and, after Goodman and Forsythe got in, topped with a foam sleeve covered in mud. John Goodman came out first and then pulled up Forsythe by the foot, the unfortunate actor's leg attached to a cable pulled by a crane to take most of the weight.

The crew also had to endure a minor uproar during shooting when the local newspaper in Tempe, Arizona, got hold of a copy of the script. The paper published a story claiming that the Coens were depicting the people of Arizona as hicks with bad taste in clothes. Ethan had to make a public defense of the film. "Of course it's not accurate," he said in exasperation. "It's not supposed to be. It's all made up. It's an Arizona of the mind." That warning was one that would apply to the settings and periods of their later films as well; they were all metaphors of consciousness rather than realistic places.

What must have been apparent from the dailies was how much warmth the sympathetic actors were bringing to a script whose intentions were largely comic. Nicolas Cage brought out Hi's vulnerability, while Holly Hunter perfectly evoked Ed's yearning for a child. While *Raising Arizona* was ostensibly about an ex-con trying to stay straight, it wasn't much of a leap to think of it as a film about anybody who tries to overcome his or her own self-destructive habits to make a better, happier life. The end of the film — when Hi and Ed return the baby and Nathan Arizona advises the forlorn couple to sleep on it before deciding to end their marriage — not only completes the film but leaves the audience with a warm feeling of comfort and satisfaction. Hi has a dream, seeing himself and Ed as an old couple being visited by their children and grandchildren, and his voice-over ends the film:

> *. . . And it seemed real. It seemed like us. And it seemed like . . . well . . . our home. . . . If not Arizona, then a land, not too far away, where all parents are strong and wise and capable, and all children are happy and beloved. . . . I dunno, maybe it was Utah.*

Did Joel and Ethan intend the dream to be a true vision of Hi and Ed's future? They didn't have to. They could let those audience members who wanted to believe it do so, while the others could just chuckle at the final joke. Barry Sonnenfeld asked Ethan whether the brothers had really meant "that stuff about love at the end." Ethan just gave Sonnenfeld a look. "I felt stupid for asking," he remembered. "I never got the answer. They are emotionally hidden."

When shooting ended — on time and on budget — the film went quickly into postproduction. This time there were no financial problems to delay the editing. The brothers could even afford to hire an editor, Michael R. Miller, although of course they leaned over his shoulder the whole time. Carter Burwell, who had done the music for *Blood Simple*, showed his versatility by creating a comic soundtrack of banjos and yodeling that underscored the unsophisticated nature of the characters and the folkloric, backwoods quality of the story. Other characters got their own themes; the biker from hell got a Spanish rock opera theme, using samples from opera singers and electric guitars. Burwell created it all in his own studio, which consisted of one sampler.

CHAPTER FIVE

GANGSTERS WITH HEART

MILLER'S CROSSING

"Nobody knows anybody. Not that well."
— Tom in *Miller's Crossing*

Because the brothers like to begin with a genre and then subvert it for their own purposes, they are hard to pinpoint or describe — and their next move is always impossible to predict. Ethan and Joel had made a pulp-fiction thriller and a near screwball comedy, having already made "a conscious effort not to repeat ourselves," as Ethan said. They weren't about to start.

The success of *Raising Arizona* would not be a factor; filmmakers are usually working on their next project, and sometimes their next two or three, well before the last one actually hits the screens. Joel and Ethan's choice of subject is not influenced by the success of the previous film simply because they don't know what that success, or lack of it, will be. In a way, this is a blessing; it allows the brothers to turn their attention to whatever interests them most at that moment. "We didn't want to do another out-and-out comedy, like *Raising Arizona*," Joel said. "We wanted to do something that was a little bit morbid.

Less of a comedy, more of a drama. We've always liked gangster movies, so it was what we started to think about when we did another script."

Actually, the brothers had been thinking about doing a gangster picture well before even writing *Raising Arizona*. They had seen a lot of classic gangster movies — including Francis Ford Coppola's *The Godfather*, whose opening they would mimic — but what really inspired them was that triumvirate of crime fiction: Cain, Hammett, and Chandler. They had already drawn on Cain for *Blood Simple*; now they wanted to try a Dashiell Hammett–like story, whose complicated plots were really just background for the story's feeling and atmosphere and characters. Their starting point was a power struggle between second-generation Italian and Irish gangs in prohibition-era America; as Ethan phrased it, "The more established Irish, the recently arrived Italians, and the sort of outsider Jews all struggling for a piece of the pie." Out of this idea rose the story of Leo, boss of the Irish syndicate running a corrupt city, and his number one assistant, Tom.

They decided not to choose a specific city, New York or Chicago say (although the story would be inspired in part by Chicago's Capone-O'Bannion gang wars), but to leave the city unnamed. "It makes the world automatically more fictional and allows you greater license in certain areas," Joel said. This is an important point for the Coens: they never have a desire to be historically accurate, to make a docudrama, or even to capture an era as it really was. They prefer to use a time and a setting only as starting points, not as limits to their imaginations. This would not prove a difficulty with *Miller's Crossing*, but it would with the next film, *Barton Fink*, when many critics would object to the way Joel and Ethan played fast and loose with its historical era. The difference may simply be that while many critics have an intellectual and emotional investment in their opinion of Hollywood in the forties and the relationship between art and political commitment, they feel no such investment in gangsters.

The story they came up with centered on the relationship of Tom Reagan to his Irish boss, Leo, who runs the town and has the mayor and the chief of police in his pocket. Despite his power, Leo would be so crazy about a woman named Verna that it would affect his judgment and allow her to manipulate him. Tom's own affair with Verna would cause a rift, sending him to Johnny Caspar, head of the rival Italian organization. Tom's defection, and a dispute over a dishonest bookie named Bernie Bernbaum (Verna's brother), would start a vicious gang war.

A good story — which it ought to have been since much of it was borrowed from Dashiell Hammett himself. While the idea of a town on the take came from Hammett's *Red Harvest,* much of the narrative was lifted from the 1931 novel *The Glass Key*. Hammett's protagonist, Ned Beaumont, became the Coens' Tom Reagan; like Ned, he would be having a bad gambling streak. He was the brothers' first really intelligent character, a man who needed to out-think everyone else and quickly, so that he was always a step ahead. "He's the quintessential Hammett guy," Joel said. "You're not let in on how much he knows and what exactly he's up to. He tests the other characters to see what they want and uses that to his advantage." Ethan added, "He's got principles and interest, and I don't think he's a pure man." They would also make him a near-alcoholic. During rehearsal Joel objected to the character leaving a glass of liquor half finished: "No, no, Tom would never leave a drink in the bottom of the glass."

The novel's crime boss, Paul Madvig, was turned into Leo — named thus because "Leo" means lion — while his rival, Shad O'Rory, became Johnny Caspar. Just as the novel's Janet had Paul wrapped around her finger, so would Leo be stupidly lovestruck by the movie's Verna. The brothers lifted lines right out of the novel and based scenes on it. They even used it as a source for all the hat imagery that would have the critics scratching their heads; Chapter Two of Hammett's novel is actually called "The Hat Trick."

All these characters — Tom, Leo, Caspar, Verna — came pretty well straight from the novel without major alteration. Perhaps the most interesting reincarnation was that of Hammett's Bernie Despain as the Coens' Bernie Bernbaum. While Hammett's character was not Jewish (at least not explicitly), the description of him comes close to some very old stereotypes of the repulsive Jew: ". . . a small man, short and stringy, with a head too large for his body. The size of his head was exaggerated until it seemed a deformity by long thick fluffy waved hair. His face was swarthy, large-featured except for the eyes. . . ." It is this description that seems to have encouraged Joel and Ethan, who, despite their own background, until now had not created a single Jewish character, to play with the stereotype themselves, much in the way that they like to play with film genres.

Writing the screenplay, Joel and Ethan didn't yet have a title and simply called it *The Bighead*, which they later said was their nickname for Tom — although it sounds more like Bernie Bernbaum. In the end a friend came up with the title

Miller's Crossing; the brothers didn't think it was great but couldn't think of anything else.

As always, they did not have the story fully worked out as they wrote, but they took Hammett's approach, which Joel described this way: "If I stir things up, I'll be able to deal with the consequences, whatever they are. Something will emerge that I can exploit." Film influences came into play, particularly Bernardo Bertolucci's *The Conformist* for the climactic forest scene, and Carol Reed's *The Third Man*, whose final scene is partially reproduced at the end of *Miller's Crossing.*

To give the screenplay a period feel and create an insulated world, the brothers drew on gangster slang. Some of it was authentic, some came from novels they had read, and some the brothers simply made up. These original expressions, such as the oft-repeated "What's the rumpus," "high hat" (meaning "disrespect"), "twist" (prostitute or easy woman), and "dangle" (to leave) have an odd effect. While clearly meant as slang, they aren't anything we've ever heard before, which gives the speeches a slight air of unreality. This invented slang is just one of the ways that the brothers undermine the apparent straight-faced intent of their story, making it impossible for many audience members to accept the film as a straightforward gangster picture. It seems as if something else is going on, although exactly what some viewers will be unsure of.

During the writing, the brothers eventually became stymied. It was not really writing block, as the press later labeled it, but simply a temporary impasse as the brothers became entangled in the intricacies of their own plot. Joel and Ethan tried writing outside their office in order to get a fresh perspective. Finally they went to St. Paul, Minnesota, and the apartment of their old friend William Preston Robertson, whose car they had commandeered back when they were making *Blood Simple.* There they hung around, drank coffee, ate donuts, and went to see lame Hollywood movies like *Baby Boom.* One night the brothers suddenly had it: not the solution to *Miller's Crossing,* but another script altogether.

Joel and Ethan returned to New York and wrote the new script, *Barton Fink,* in three weeks. Then they finished *Miller's Crossing,* thus ending what may have turned out to be the most productive writer's block in film history.

The screenplay of *Miller's Crossing* opens with Johnny Caspar, sitting across from the city's leading crime boss Leo, giving a speech about honor among

Albert Finney and Gabriel Byrne as Dashiell Hammett characters reinvented in *Miller's Crossing*   EVERETT COLLECTION

thieves. He has come to tell Leo about his intention to kill Bernie Bernbaum for selling information about fixed fights, but Leo refuses to give Caspar permission. Tom, Leo's right-hand man, thinks Leo is making a "bad play" in getting Caspar angry, but Leo brushes off the concern. Some time later Leo wakes up Tom in his apartment, worried because he doesn't know where Verna is. Tom tries to warn Leo off her ("... if she's such an angel why are you looking for her at four in the morning?") but Leo is too smitten to listen. After he leaves, Tom goes into the bedroom, where we see none other than Verna herself in Tom's bed. Tom is disgusted with Verna because he thinks she is Leo's girl only to protect her brother, Bernie.

Leo thinks that the alleyway murder of one of his henchmen, Rug Daniels, is a hit by Johnny Caspar to show Leo he means business. Leo responds by calling in the mayor and the police chief and ordering them to close down Caspar's illegal drinking and gambling parlors. Realizing that Leo is starting a gangster war just to protect Verna's brother, Tom finds Verna in the ladies lounge of Leo's club and asks her to stop influencing Leo. Their tough-talking sparring — she socks him in the jaw, he throws his drink at her — may show that Tom and Verna actually love one another but can't admit it.

Tom is visited in his apartment by Bernie, who, like almost everyone else, wants to help Tom out with his gambling debts in order to have Tom on his side. Then Johnny Caspar asks Tom to visit, but when Tom refuses to, he has his boys work Tom over. Then the police burst in, sent by Leo to break up Caspar's racket. Tom goes to see Verna at her apartment and she tries to get him to drop his emotional guard. "Admit you don't like me seeing Leo because you're jealous. Admit it isn't all cool calculation with you — that you've got a heart — even if it's small and feeble and you can't remember the last time you used it." Perhaps if Tom did admit his feelings the story would turn out differently, but he keeps his defenses up, although the two go to bed together anyway.

Caspar sends his men to kill Leo in his house, but in a bravura performance of gangster skill, Leo turns one of their own machine guns on them and comes out alive, although his house is in flames. Tom believes that Leo no longer appears strong and won't be able to hold the city unless he gives Bernie up to Caspar. But when Leo still refuses because of Verna, whom he wants to marry, Tom makes a sacrifice of himself by admitting that he and Verna are sleeping together. Leo punches Tom in the face and one of his men throws Tom down the stairs.

After another night with Verna, Tom goes over to Caspar's side; only later will it become clear that he is doing this to save Leo. Tom tells Caspar where to find Bernie, but his plan seems to backfire when Caspar sends Tom out with his men to pick Bernie up and then murder him under the trees of Miller's Crossing. As Tom and Bernie stumble through the woods, Bernie pleads for his life. In a moment of weakness — or heart — Tom lets Bernie go, only pretending to kill him, telling him never to return.

Meanwhile, the war between Leo and Caspar continues, tearing up the city. Bernie, who was supposed to leave town, shows up in Tom's apartment, having decided to take advantage of his savior's moment of weakness. When Caspar's thug the Dane finds out that Bernie might be alive, he picks up Tom and takes him back to Miller's Crossing. If there's no body to be found Tom himself will soon be lying under the trees. But a decomposing body is found — it is Mink, murdered by his clandestine lover Bernie — and Tom has used up one more of his nine lives.

Caspar has taken over the city; now the mayor and the police are in *his* pocket. Thinking overtime, Tom manages to get Caspar to believe that the Dane has been double-crossing him in order to take over the operation. Verna, who has been told by the Dane that Tom whacked her brother for Caspar, tries to kill Tom but doesn't have it in her to pull the trigger. But their romance is over. Caspar is shot to death by Bernie in a complicated setup arranged by Tom, after which Tom arrives and, instead of helping Bernie out, shoots him dead. So much for his one weak moment. The screenplay ends with Bernie's Jewish funeral. After Verna leaves, Tom and Leo talk one last time and Leo asks Tom to come back to work for him. Tom refuses.

It was the most complex plot the brothers had yet devised, so it is not surprising that it took them some time to work out. And making it work on the screen would be their biggest challenge yet.

Working in the System

With the script of *Miller's Crossing* finished, the brothers knew they had upped the ante again. The budget for a period film like this one was going to be another leap from that of *Raising Arizona*, which was a leap from *Blood Simple*. But Twentieth Century Fox, which had put up half the budget for *Raising Arizona*, had made a decent profit, and just as importantly, the Coen brothers now had an established reputation as innovative filmmakers with a promising future. While most decisions in the end come down to money and risk, film studio executives are not immune to other forces. And prestige filmmakers like Joel and Ethan were just the sort to give a studio a reputation for daring, artful filmmaking.

In fact, Fox wasn't the only one to want the picture; so did other studios, such as Universal, where Jim Jacks, formerly of Circle Releasing, now worked. But Ben Barenholtz had already worked a deal with Fox before the script was written, based on a mere two-line description of the project. Fox had the first right of refusal; they could agree to finance it or turn it down. And that was all. They could not have any influence on the script whatsoever, or on the finished film, unless the Coens decided to substantially change the submitted script. Barenholtz said, "It's a unique deal. And it shows that there is room to work within the system and get good films made." Fox read the script and agreed to put up the full budget, reported in the industry at $14 million (the brothers claimed it was ten). Jim Jacks could only shrug at not getting the film for Universal; as he put it, even though the film was by no means a guaranteed profit-maker, it would be a "black eye for the company to let these guys get away." And Jacks made a farsighted prediction. One day, he said, "the Coens will write a script that they think is off-center, and between the time they write it and it comes out, the center will have moved just enough that they will hit it right in the middle, and they will be appalled." That is just what would happen with *Fargo*.

Casting a period film was a trickier business than casting a contemporary one; the actors had to seem believable to the audience, as if they really did belong to an earlier time. As Tom, the brothers had expected to cast an American actor since the character was intended to be of Irish descent but American born. For this reason, the Irish actor Gabriel Byrne, suggested for the part by casting agent Donna Isaacson, intended to read for his audition with an American accent. Although he was an admirer of the brothers, they had little idea who he was. And the truth was, Byrne was known more for being the husband of Ellen Barkin than for anything else. Pale-skinned, with very dark hair and piercing blue eyes, he was handsome in a real, hard-earned way, perhaps because his crooked nose had been broken four times. Byrne had come to acting late, after working as a messenger, bartender, factory worker, and teacher, joining Dublin's Abbey Theatre at the age of 29. His first film role was in John Boorman's *Excalibur*, but most of the films he had been in since, including *Siesta* with his wife, had been flops. For better or worse he liked offbeat directors and unusual scripts — no wonder the Coens appealed to him.

Reading the script, Byrne found the language "a joy to listen to." It felt more like a theater piece to him than a movie and, reading it aloud, he thought, "My God, this could have been written by somebody from Dublin." And so when he went into the audition he asked to read in his natural Irish lilt. Joel and Ethan were skeptical — making Tom an immigrant would shift the film's dynamics — but they agreed and liked what they heard. But to Byrne they seemed cryptically passive and he went away not knowing what impression he had made. Not for eight weeks did he find out that he had won the role.

For Leo, the brothers had already decided on Trey Wilson, the actor who had played Nathan Arizona in *Raising Arizona*. Leo's nemesis, Johnny Caspar, was intended to be a man in his fifties, so actor Jon Polito, who was only in his thirties, had to convince the Coens he was right for it. A New York stage actor, he had won an OBIE Award for performing in five different plays in a single season. He had starred in Dustin Hoffman's famous revival of *Death of a Salesman* (later filmed for CBS), and had appeared in several television shows and films. He was not a star but a busy, working actor, who had already played some gangster roles. The Coens gave in, making *Miller's Crossing* just the first of their pictures that Polito would appear in.

Perhaps a more difficult part to fill was that of Verna, the only significant female role in a film about an insular male world. (This was just the first of the pictures, including *Barton Fink* and *The Big Lebowski*, the brothers have made about predominantly male societies.) When Joel's wife, Frances McDormand, read the script, she thought it was great; and she wanted to play Verna. Since being discovered by the Coens and moving in with Joel, McDormand had not had as much film work as might be expected. She had appeared in some television shows as well as on- and off-Broadway theater, and had received a Tony nomination for her portrait of Stella in a production of *A Streetcar Named Desire*. But she had only been in one non–Coen brothers film, *Mississippi Burning*, although for her work as a beauty parlor assistant who stands up to white racists she would earn an Academy Award nomination for best supporting actress. To her the role of Verna seemed just what her acting career needed. But when she mentioned the part to Joel he just replied, "Yeah, we're going to start casting for it." That he didn't wish to even consider her was difficult for McDormand to accept. She did take on a small uncredited role as a secretary, but at some point she and Joel had to "work it out," McDormand herself later admitted.

Possibly one of the reasons for not casting McDormand, besides perhaps feeling that she wasn't right for the part, was that the brothers liked to find unknowns for their female leads. First there was McDormand herself, followed by Holly Hunter. Would they be able to discover another not-yet-famous female actor and make her a name? Marcia Gay Harden was certainly unknown. The daughter of a U.S. Navy captain, she had fallen for acting on seeing ancient Greek plays performed in open amphitheaters in Greece where her father was stationed. A graduate of the University of Texas drama department, she had moved to New York to look for work. So far she had acted only in theater, albeit in plays by several of the great modernist playwrights — Chekhov, Brecht,

Pinter, and Sam Shepard. Frustrated by her lack of success, she had decided to go back to school — in this case New York University. And it was there, in a school production of *A Comedy of Errors*, that she was spotted by the eagle-eyed casting agent Donna Isaacson. As Verna, she would later be aptly described by David Denby in *New York* as a "hard-knocks girl" with a "beautiful ugly face."

The casting went on. J.E. Freeman, a hardworking journeyman actor, was chosen as the Dane, the ruthless right-hand man to Johnny Caspar. Steve Buscemi, a Brooklyn-born actor with limp hair, a morose-looking face, and ungainly teeth, was cast in the small part of Mink, the Dane's lover, beginning a long association with the Coens as one of their continuing "company." But it was another role, much smaller than it seemed but demanding a bravura performance, upon which the film would really depend. Bernie Bernbaum.

In the theater world there is a term for the character who serves as a catalyst for the dramatic action: fifth business. And Bernie Bernbaum was definitely the fifth business of *Miller's Crossing*, the bookie without "ethics" (as Caspar puts it) who sells information on fixed fights to make an additional profit. John Turturro, cast in the role, said of Bernie, "He's much more verbal and intellectual [than his previous roles]. He's dangerous, but more with his mind and his mouth." Turturro also called him "a devilish character," a "phantom," and noted that "all my scenes are with Tom, so I really exist through him."

Born in Brooklyn to Italian immigrants, Turturro went to the State University of New York before receiving a master's degree from the Yale School of Drama. He made his brief screen debut in Martin Scorsese's *Raging Bull* before going on to off-Broadway and regional theater. He made a name for himself in the John Patrick Shanley play *Danny & the Deep Blue Sea*. Then came film roles: *To Live and Die in L.A.*, *The Color of Money*, *Five Corners*. But his breakthrough came as the bigoted son in Spike Lee's *Do the Right Thing*, a remarkably real performance that humanized the character without softening him. "He's not concerned whether people are gonna like his character at all, and that's important," Lee once said of him. Perhaps that was why Turturro was willing to play the character of the Jewish club owner in Lee's *Mo' Better Blues*, a role that resulted in Lee being condemned by Jewish organizations and some critics as anti-Semitic.

Turturro, whose wife happens to be Jewish, seems to have been disturbed by these charges, feeling that his part was altered in the editing room. This did not

John Turturro based his portrait of Bernie Bernbaum on his accountant and the devil   PATTI PERRETT/PHOTOFEST

stop him, however, from jumping at the chance to play Bernie, another unappealing and morally dubious Jewish character. Quite likely he felt the role was too good to pass up, as was the chance to work with the Coen brothers. And the fact that Joel and Ethan were Jewish seemed to make the character more acceptable. Perhaps the more interesting question is, why did the brothers choose Turturro? Why would they, like Lee, choose a non-Jewish actor for the role when a Jewish actor might have been more convincing to the audience? Did they actually hope to trade on the fresh memory of Turturro's earlier performance in the Spike Lee film, so that the audience might bring negative feelings to the character of Bernie? Was it because Turturro's physical appearance — his oddly shaped head, his small eyes, his notable nose — played to certain old stereotypes of the ugly Jew, making him another Shylock or Fagin? After all, the brothers had a fondness for playing with genres and types. In what would become known as the famous begging scene, when Bernie is pleading with Tom not to kill him, Joel and Ethan wrote dialogue for the bookie that might have come out of Shakespeare or Dickens: "I couldn't help it, Tom, it's my nature.

Somebody hands me an angle, I play it. I don't deserve to die for that!" A Jew, Bernie implies, cannot be blamed for simply acting according to his nature. It seems that the two Jewish boys from Minneapolis wanted to stare unblinkingly into the ancient image of the Jewish moneylender. And whereas it is possible to find redeeming human values in both Shylock and Fagin, Bernie Bernbaum has none. He is unscrupulous, greedy, morally degenerate (especially in how he uses his sister Verna), and cowardly.

Interestingly, Turturro himself seems to have been divided about the character. At times he sounded almost like an apologist, claiming that "He's a guy who's just trying to be a survivor. He's constantly on the move, which is kind of Jewish history." At other times he clearly saw Bernie as an unrelievedly evil figure: "He's almost like the devil. I think that Joel and Ethan were inspired by Faust."

Casting of the film seemed to be set until sudden tragedy struck. Trey Wilson, prepared to play Leo, had a brain hemorrhage and died two days before the first day of scheduled shooting. The brothers had to recast the part, and quickly. They had always liked Albert Finney, a large actor with a strong physical presence but also a genuine warmth to him. By chance, the actor happened to be available.

Albert Finney was born in 1936, in an industrial area of Northern England. He graduated from the Royal Academy of Dramatic Arts in London along with Peter O'Toole and Alan Bates, turning down film roles to do Shakespeare. His film debut came in *The Entertainer* in 1960, followed by acclaim in *Saturday Night and Sunday Morning* and *Tom Jones*. While he had made many movies since, including the more recent *Under the Volcano* and *The Dresser*, he had dedicated most of his career to the stage. But he had seen *Raising Arizona* when it opened and considered the brothers to be among the more interesting young filmmakers around. While the script of *Miller's Crossing* seemed somewhat cartoonlike to him, especially in its violence, he admired its tremendous craftsmanship. Following Byrne's example, he decided to use an Irish accent for the role, underscoring the immigrant-warfare theme of the film.

The rest of preproduction continued. Barry Sonnenfeld, whose success with the earlier Coen brothers films had by then gotten him jobs on *Big*, *Throw Momma from the Train*, and *When Harry Met Sally*, worked with the brothers and artist J. Todd Anderson on the all-important storyboards. The violent set pieces and period detail had to be precisely worked out in order to keep to the tight budget. He and the brothers decided to use a shallow-focus lens rather than the wide-angle lenses they preferred for the previous films. This time the audience would have its gaze more directed to the focused point on the screen. In a film with more talk, the viewer, they decided, had to know where to look. Sonnenfeld also decided to use a different film for the outdoor forest scenes — Fuji instead of Kodak for its softer, more muted greens. Dennis Gassner, who had begun as a record-album designer and cut his teeth at Francis Ford Coppola's Zoetrope Studios before it went under, signed on as the production designer. He found a visual theme for the film in columns — an architectural equivalent to the trees in the woods at Miller's Crossing — and asked for locations to be scouted that had them. He also wanted to control the color scheme of the film more than had been done in the earlier Coen brothers works. Richard Hornung, who had done the costumes for *Raising Arizona*, created a "thug uniform" for the gangsters — soft-shouldered jackets, nipped-in waists, hats with broad brims to shadow faces. Most of these details were true to the period; only the big coats were not accurate. But Hornung knew that it wasn't really authenticity the brothers were going for. "My theory with the Coens," he said, "is always that the costume is approved if they laugh." He flew Marcia Gay Harden to New Orleans for a costume fitting that went on for hours. Her clothes were not quite in the boxy masculine style of the era, but rather more slinky. She herself tried to come up with her make-up, giving herself strong eyebrows and a bold mouth. But the brothers thought she looked too vampirish and softened it.

This time the rehearsal period was only a week long. When Jon Polito tried out his long and very funny opening monologue about the nature of ethics among gangsters, the brothers listened and then, in unison, told him that he missed a word. As for what the speech meant to the brothers and how they wanted him to deliver it — on those points they were silent. Marcia Gay Harden, experienced on the stage but not before the cameras, found that she, like the other actors, had to focus mostly on how much of her feelings to reveal and how much to hide. Shooting the scenes out of sequential order — an almost universal practice in filmmaking, in order to make more efficient use of setups and locations — ended up being less daunting than many theater actors expect. "Modern plays aren't sequential either," she noted. "Anyone who has ever done a flashback on stage knows you have to hold the entire plot line in your head all the time."

. Perhaps the actor who had to work the hardest, and take the largest risks, to find his character was John Turturro. Turturro himself admitted that he was "neurotic" about preparing for the role. He decided, strangely, to pattern his performance on a real person — a Jewish man named Abe who happened to be his accountant. Strange, because Turturro called Abe a "wonderfully sweet man"; nevertheless, he used him for "the way he walks, the way he holds his shoulders, the way he laughs — *huh, huh, huh.*" He even asked Abe to translate his lines into Yiddish so that he could hear them with a more Jewish inflection; if anything, Turturro wanted to play up Bernie's Jewishness. In the film, Bernie's movements have an odd, almost birdlike quality in the way he swivels his head and moves his arms. And his walk is a kind of tick-tock sideways movement that evokes that old Shylock/Fagin stereotype of the awkward, physically unnatural Jew. Richard Hornung's deviously clever costume — a derby hat, a long square-cut coat reminiscent of Hasidic garb, and a white frilled scarf like a prayer shawl — would emphasize this image.

An Actor's Humiliation

"New Orleans is sort of a depressed city," Ethan said to explain their choice to film *Miller's Crossing* there after visiting several cities with line producer Graham Place. "It hasn't been gentrified. There's a lot of architecture that hasn't been touched, storefront windows that haven't been replaced in the past 60 years." Many buildings from the 1920s remain virtually unchanged. Another good reason to choose the city was that Joel and Ethan wanted a gray, moody look for the film; they had decided to shoot in the winter but didn't want snow.

Next, the brothers worked with Dennis Gassner, location manager Amy Ness, and a local scout to find the actual sites. For Leo's club they chose the International House, a private club whose members had never allowed filming before. Rug Daniels would have his life ended behind an old gate; the cops would shoot it out with Leo's men on Church Street. Both Johnny Caspar's office and the mayor's office would be shot in the old city hall. Sets that had to be built, such as Tom's apartment — meant to metaphorically convey "the inside of Tom's head" — were built in a garage on Annunciation Street. (This notion of a room as a metaphor for the mind would be carried out to greater extremes in *Barton Fink*.) And finally, a tree farm 90 minutes away would become the forest of Miller's Crossing.

And so the shoot began. "It wasn't a fun set to be on at all," Gabriel Byrne said afterwards. "People were there to work really hard." He did, however, take a moment to crack up the set by performing his lines in a Humphrey Bogart accent; Byrne had drawn on the tough but wounded Bogart persona for his performance. Perhaps for Byrne fun was lacking because he had to endure his character being repeatedly punched, roughed up, thrown down stairs, and generally abused. Most distressing was being strangled by Jon Polito playing Johnny Caspar. "If you're ever doing a strangling scene, don't do it with a method actor," Byrne warned. "This guy was totally into it. There were blood vessels ready to burst all over my face." Byrne also noted how "modest" and "unassuming" the brothers were and how deceptive was their youthful appearance. "It was like making a movie with the guys down the road in their back garden. Sometimes you felt you ought to go up and check there was film in the camera." The inexperienced Marcia Gay Harden said that making the film was like "being in school and the principal is this really young guy your age."

As usual, the brothers stuck pretty closely to the storyboards, especially for the action sequences. And it was true that the brothers did not enjoy having their dialogue messed around with. "I don't think most actors think it's particularly remarkable that we stick to the script," Ethan said in defense of their rigidity. "The reason they work with us in the first place is not usually the money. It's because they like the script." Barry Sonnenfeld said of the brothers, "They do everything. They write it, they cast it, they work on the editing, they're involved with the music. They don't hire people to go out and do these things. They are so insularly self-confident, it doesn't matter what anyone else thinks." The brothers were willing, however, to take suggestions for movement in the dialogue scenes. As well, since Joel and Ethan weren't the sort to offer much direction, the actors had room to interpret the words they were given to say. Turturro explained, "Sometimes a [director] can say everything and you don't get anything. Other times, people can just be there and go through it with you and you get it. The Coens are like that." He found them interested in seeing what he might do differently on the fifth or sixth take. "Once or twice I threw in a new thing by accident, and they liked it. I think I've surprised them a few times." Other actors discovered that Joel and Ethan had their own subtle ways of getting an actor to play a scene their way. Jon Polito found the brothers' approach "deceptive. They sort of giggle and make you laugh along with them, until finally you realize you're going in a way they planned years before. They have a wonderful way of catching you off guard."

One of the various strands of the story that the actors themselves found most mysterious was the hat imagery. The opening shot, of a hat being blown through the woods, was filmed in the tree farm outside the city. Richard Hornung designed an "everyman's hat" for the shot; it was not intended to belong to a specific character. Specially made to be lightweight, it was attached to a fishing line that made it appear to be carried off by the wind. The shot, actually the last filmed, was the first image that came to the brothers while they were writing, without, as Ethan said, "really knowing how it was supposed to fit in." Gabriel Byrne thought about the meaning of hats during the shoot. During one conversation with Verna, he speaks of dreaming about his hat blowing away in the woods. When Verna cynically asks him whether it turned into "something wonderful," Tom says no, it stayed a hat. "It was really weird that nobody mentioned the hat all the way through the movie," Byrne said later. "I said to Joel at one point, 'What is the significance of the hat? Is the hat significant?' And he said, 'Mmm hmm.' And that was it."

In fact, it seems quite possible that neither Joel nor Ethan could have answered Byrne's question, before, during, or after the shoot. Ethan: "I mean, the whole hat thing, the fact that it's all hats, is good, because even if it doesn't mean anything, it adds a little thread running through the whole thing that's the same little thread." A symbol, then, that has no actual symbolic meaning? That is intuitive and not rational? This will not be the last time that the brothers will include such possibly empty symbols in their work — the box that Charlie Meadows gives Barton Fink is another. The result makes the films more mysterious and subject to interpretation. Here the hats may represent Tom's sense of the precariousness of life, or of a man's dignity, which can be so easily lost — but neither of these feels fully satisfying. This impossibility of interpretation can also have the effect — perhaps intended — of making the films seem strangely hollow at the center, as if something is missing. They feel like opening a beautifully wrapped package only to find it empty inside.

The most difficult, time-consuming, and expensive sequence to shoot was certainly the attempted hit on Leo at his house. It is a long and wordless sequence — a trademark element of every Coen brothers film — that allows the brothers, and especially Joel, to show off their visual flare. It allowed for great stylization, as well as references to film tradition going back to the films of James Cagney. Another of its purposes was to break up all the dialogue. "It's about time at that point to shed a little blood," was how Ethan put it. Also, it revealed how tough Leo was, able to defeat four would-be assassins. He was vulnerable and weak only when it came to Verna. From the beginning they imagined the sequence playing ironically to the sound of the sentimental Irish ballad "Danny Boy," which they had sung by Frank Patterson, the Irish tenor who acted and sang in John Huston's *The Dead.* Thinking more in film terms than in reality, Ethan said, "It isn't intended to be riotously funny, but there's something . . . *fun* about it. It's a Big Death, you know?"

The sequence was actually shot at several different locations, including studio interior sets, over several weeks. Leo, smoking a cigar as he lies on his bed, first notices something is going on — the assassins downstairs have killed his guards — when he sees wisps of smoke coming up through the floorboards. (This is another image that will be elaborated upon in *Barton Fink.*) It was particularly difficult to film Leo rolling beneath his bed to protect himself from machine-gun fire. An elevated set had to be built in order for the camera to shoot eye-level with Leo under the bed. Squibs were set off in the mattress above the actor while an airgun was used to fire feathers downwards on him.

The second assassin was the one who got to perform what is known in movies as the "Thompson jitterbug," named after the kind of machine gun the gangsters always used. The actor, Monte Starr, performed for the front shot, but a stunt double was used to show the gunman's body "dancing" jerkily as it is riddled with bullets. The double was needed because a real machine gun is heavy and it is hard for a regular actor to perform the dance while his own gun is firing off and recoiling and squibs are going off on his back. While filming the scene, the brothers added little violent flourishes, such as the gunman spraying his own feet with lead. "It was a lot of fun blowing the toes off," Joel said. "The only regret is that it goes by so fast, you almost kind of miss it. They're a highlight."

If the assassin sequence was the most difficult technically to shoot, surely the most difficult emotionally was Bernie Bernbaum's begging scene. Hired on by Johnny Caspar after splitting with Leo, Tom is given the job of taking Bernie into the woods and putting two bullets into him. The words that Joel and Ethan wrote ("You *can't* kill me. I'm praying to you! Look in your heart! I'm praying to you! Look in your heart!") seem to have a tortured desperateness to them as, throwing all dignity aside, Bernie begs not to die. This scene, too, plays on Bernie's Jewishness; he is a person not of physical action but of words, using crafty rhetoric rather than force to save himself. It is the Coens' equivalent of Shylock's famous "If you prick us, do we not bleed?" speech.

The scene was equally important for Tom's character, even though Gabriel Byrne had to resort to very restrained acting techniques. "All through the picture, Tom is battling with the idea of love and the idea of giving himself to another person," he said. "The turning point for Tom is at Miller's Crossing. Bernie gets through to his heart and he lets go. From then on everything goes haywire, and he determines never again to be ruled by his heart."

On the day of filming it was cold and Turturro, only in shirtsleeves, found himself freezing and his nose running. The brothers let him decide how to play the scene and Turturro chose to let down all his defenses and be "as human as possible." "Great acting," he explained, "has to do with self-exposure." Something of a method actor, he decided to draw on a remembered personal experience. When he was seventeen, coming home late from a party one night with some friends, he found himself with an off-duty cop's gun pressed to his head. The fear of that moment fed his performance of terror, hysteria, and abject humility.

Seeing the raw footage afterwards, Joel and Ethan worried about how Turturro would feel seeing the depths of humiliation he reached up on the screen. But it was a great performance, the most memorable in the film, and they knew it.

Critical Success, Public Miss

In postproduction, the brothers called on Michael Miller once more for the hands-on editing work. But another editor, Tricia Cooke, also worked on the film. She and Ethan would begin to see one another; in 1992, they would marry. After *Miller's Crossing*, she would work on all their films.

Carter Burwell was called in, as always, for the music. While he used some traditional Irish music, some of it suggested by Gabriel Byrne, Burwell had to write the film's thematic score — the first orchestral music he had ever written.

Gabriel Byrne with the Coen brothers at the Independent Spirit
Awards, 1997   LEE SALEM/SHOOTING STAR

"That's certainly one of the nicer things about working with Joel and Ethan," he
said. "They really enjoy asking people to do things they haven't done before."
What he came up with was grand, dark, mournful, romantic, and beautifully
melodic — by far his best work to date. Like all great film music, it would not
merely complement what was on the screen but would actually give the images
greater emotional depth and resonance. It heightened the emotional, human
story and the period feel rather than playing to the film's ironic side.

At the time of *Miller's Crossing*'s release in the fall of 1990, the brothers
were still living in New York, and still avoiding celebrity events. If he had to
go to a party, Ethan was known to take a book with him. He was now 33; Joel
was 35. They had already shot their next film, *Barton Fink*, and were hardly
thinking about *Miller's Crossing* anymore. It was chosen to open the New York
Film Festival, and then was screened in Washington to benefit FilmFest DC. As
a matter of obligation, the brothers went to the Washington post-screening
party, where they were described by a journalist: "Looking more like guys who

spend too much time at the movies than guys who make them, they didn't work particularly hard at feigning indifference, sequestering themselves at a corner table."

With good advance word, the film got plenty of press. Articles and profiles of the actors asked such questions as, would *Miller's Crossing* finally make Gabriel Byrne into a major star? (In the end, it wouldn't.) A feature in the popular film magazine *Premiere* called it "the single most impressive movie of the year so far." It was, the writer proclaimed, "a brilliant mixture of satire and seriousness, style and substance, a bitter love story embedded in a gangster gothic, a film that is at once an homage to films noir past and an extraordinarily assured leap into the future." The Coens had "dropped their ironic distance" for once to make a film with heart. This, the writer asserted, was the Coens' first film that wasn't about film itself but about "humanity."

It was a position that many of the positive reviews took. The Coens had shown an icy stylishness in *Blood Simple*, a goofy if unserious charm in *Raising Arizona*, and finally had reached a genuine depth of feeling in *Miller's Crossing*. "This time," wrote the critic for *Rolling Stone*, "they're not just showing off their technique. There's a new self-assurance with no loss of wit or invention. Instead of merely looking for ways to send up the crime genre, the Coens are searching for its heart. . . . [It is] their most impassioned film." The well-known film critic Jay Scott of the Toronto *Globe and Mail* also felt this heart, although his reading of it was darker; ". . . a masterpiece, but of a unique kind," he called it. "It's a gangster movie so morally and ethically bleak, it evokes the dead-end world of the ultimate twentieth-century playwright, Samuel Beckett; lower or higher than this, you cannot go."

But such critics, while certainly appreciating aspects of the film, had almost willfully blinded themselves to its more playful, ironic, self-reflexive side. They wanted to be moved by the story and characters, and they were. Other critics, however, were more in tune with the Coens' strange sense of fun. David Denby in *New York* declared the film "perverse and wonderful," with "the richest, darkest texture of melancholy that we've seen in recent American movies. . . . Yet the Coens, as always, are joking. *Miller's Crossing* hides within the folds of its dark-toned magnificence an anarchic brand of fun. . . . What matters to the Coens is not what a gangster is really like but the fabulous ways he can be represented."

Unfortunately, critics like Denby who saw the Coens' subversive side had trouble taking the love story as seriously as the critics who responded more emotionally. Denby, for one, found the Tom-Verna scenes to be weak points because they felt "synthetic." It was as if Joel and Ethan had tried to be serious while at the same time being unable to take their own seriousness, well, seriously. Was *Miller's Crossing* a solemn love story or a secret comedy? Was Tom a "genuine" character, a silently suffering stoic who learned, if for just a moment, to open his heart, or was he merely a clever amalgam of earlier gangster-novel and film heroes? For most critics, it wasn't possible to be both. Not all critics who saw the same cleverness that Denby did appreciated it. Vincent Canby in the *New York Times* panned the film, calling it all style and no substance. In fact, this was one of the few negative reviews that the brothers ever responded to. Joel replied with a simple assertion that Canby was not on their wavelength: "[The review is] not decipherable in terms of our own thought process." Bill Brownstein of the *Montreal Gazette* had a mirror-opposite response to that of *Premiere:* "It's devilishly ironic and intelligent, but it has no heart. The Coens do their darndest to distance themselves from their audience, and they succeed." And Terrence Rafferty, the *New Yorker's* new critic, replacing Pauline Kael, noted the irony but not the warmth. "This is not so much a gangster movie as an extended, elaborate allusion to one."

While this handful of dour critics could not feel any enthusiasm for the film, there was one who was not just negative but angry. He was Gary Giddins in the *Village Voice;* his condemnation of the film as a largely formal exercise was only a kind of warm-up. What really maddened Giddins was the film's "gratuitous fag- and yid-bashing," which he claimed was much worse than Spike Lee's controversial film *Mo' Better Blues.* He noted that the film's three homosexual characters — the Dane (a murderous thug), Mink (a "cowering pansy"), and Bernie Bernbaum — were the most reprehensible and repulsive in the film. And as for Bernie — "If the guardians of Jewish publicity think Spike Lee resurrected stereotypes of anti-Semitism, what will they make of this sniveling, money-mad horror?"

In fact, the Coens would not have to face the charge of using Jewish stereotypes — at least not until their next film. And as for the gay characters in *Miller's Crossing,* it was a shame that Giddins noticed only the overt ones. It is easy to read a gay subtext in the relationship between Tom and Leo. Tom's seduction of Verna can be seen as a hidden way of reaching Leo, or as a jealous response to her. In the end, Tom's only real loyalty is not to Verna but to Leo. And Leo's final speech, when he tries to convince Tom to work for him again, sounds like a man trying to convince a lover to return:

> *Jesus, Tom! I'd give anything if you'd work for me again. I know I've made some bonehead plays! I know I can be pig-headed, but, damnit, so can you! I need your help, and things can be like they were, I know it! I just know it!*

It's possible that this subtext was inspired by Bertolucci's *The Conformist*, an admitted inspiration for the film, which concerns a repressed homosexual. It is also possible that the homosexual subtext is a metaphor for another kind of love between men — brotherly love. In any case, intelligently judging the Jewish or the homosexual characters in *Miller's Crossing* would certainly involve more than just responding to them as evocations of stereotypes.

Despite the articles and profiles, the slew of positive reviews, even the potential controversy, *Miller's Crossing* failed to draw an audience, falling considerably behind the success of *Raising Arizona*. Part of the reason must have been the near-simultaneous release of three other violent gangster films: *The Godfather* III, *State of Grace*, and Martin Scorsese's chilling masterpiece, *Goodfellas*. Possibly it was also the Coens' insistence on walking that line between sincerity and irony. While film aficionados might like this sort of game, the average moviegoer does not enjoy being confused about his or her responses.

To their credit, Joel and Ethan did not measure their own sense of a film's success or failure by its box office. Nor did they find it so easy to imagine the mass audience out there. Joel said, "It does become really abstract. Theoretically you made the movie for other people to watch, it's for an audience, so you want as many people as possible. . . . But after it reaches a certain point, it's really weird to differentiate whether a million and a half or three million see it." On the other hand, it was also true that financial success meant more freedom to make the films they envisioned. *Raising Arizona* had opened the door to bigger budgets; they could only hope that the failure of *Miller's Crossing* would not close it again. And surely they must have been worried about their next film, already in the can. For if a gangster picture with love and violence could fail, what could the future be for a movie about a left-wing writer who goes to Hollywood and suffers writer's block?

CHAPTER SIX

THE
WALLPAPER MOVIE

BARTON FINK

"Look, it's really just a formula.
You don't have to type your soul into it."
— Audrey in *Barton Fink*

While Joel and Ethan are notoriously — and frustratingly — elusive with American journalists, they are sometimes willing to reveal more to interviewers from Europe. Perhaps it is because their films do well overseas, where audiences have often embraced the more avant-garde American filmmakers, or that European critics take film more seriously as an art and ask more interesting questions. Whatever the reason, it was to an interviewer from a French journal that the brothers explained they hadn't really been suffering from writer's block during the writing of *Miller's Crossing*. Rather, at a certain point they needed some distance from the story in order to get more perspective on the plot entanglements they had created. So they took a break, and during it they wrote another screenplay with surprising speed.

Joel and Ethan had been reading about the history of moviemaking in the thirties and forties, the period of the big studio system when stars and writers were kept on contract by the Jewish moguls who had essentially founded Hollywood. The book that primarily ignited their interest was *City of Nets: A Portrait of Hollywood in the 1940s* by Otto Friedrich, a history with a special interest in German expatriates in Los Angeles. While the brothers claimed to have no special interest in the period, they thought it might be interesting to use it for a story of their own as what Joel called the "background element." Later Ethan would say, "that's almost the cheapest part of the movie. Some of it was fun to write and hopefully fun to see, but it's not really what we were interested in — we just threw a little in for good measure." This casual attitude wasn't really different from the way the brothers felt about the history of gangsters in America when writing *Miller's Crossing* or the criminal justice system when writing *Raising Arizona;* they were quite happy to use what they knew, invent what they didn't, and change what they wanted to. But, as we shall see, while the critics accepted this sort of play in the earlier films, some of them took considerable exception to it in *Barton Fink.* Hollywood, politics, and Jews, it would turn out, were a potent — and controversial — combination.

In any case, Hollywood was not in fact the starting place for the screenplay's conception. The first image that Joel and Ethan had was of the actors John Goodman and John Turturro sitting on a hotel bed in their underwear. (Did this image have homosexual connotations? Or did it evoke a distant memory of two young brothers getting dressed in the morning?) In fact, they were so set on John Goodman not just playing, but "being" the role that they imagined that they took the actor out for dinner and ran the idea past him before writing the script. They also spoke to Turturro, for whom they wanted to write a major role and whose character — the more passively responsive one as they imagined it — was equally essential. These two characters were to both live in "a big seedy hotel" as Joel described it, and the reason for Turturro's presence came from their reading; he would be a left-wing Jewish writer, something like the real writer Clifford Odets, brought to Hollywood to write for the pictures.

Perhaps it was the complications of *Miller's Crossing,* with its multiple settings and characters, that made them want to write a much "smaller" film, set almost entirely in a single room, and dominated by its two main characters. Quite likely it was also the experience of creating Bernie Bernbaum, their first Jewish character, that piqued their interest in exploring two other Jewish stereotypes: the committed writer and the Hollywood mogul. They may have even been thinking of their own position as artists who also were Jews and where they might — or might not — fit in. For although they were Jewish in origin and upbringing, their films up to this point pointedly steered away from any content that reflected this aspect of themselves. Their films were about Southerners, the Irish, Italians — but not Jews. Other Jewish filmmakers, like Jewish novelists and playwrights, had often engaged themselves in social issues. But the brothers? Well, they were just trying to entertain people and themselves. Did this make them somehow decadent or merely superficial? It is possible to read the character of Barton Fink as their answer — a committed writer who turns out to be pompous, naïve, absolutely self-involved, fearful, and cold. Perhaps John Goodman's character running through the burning hotel, firing a shotgun and bellowing, "I'll show you the life of the mind!" is the brothers' answer to the value of "committed" art.

As always with Joel and Ethan, there were also some strong film influences at work. First and foremost was Roman Polanski, whose morally creepy and sexually uneasy works could leave audiences feeling haunted for days. Joel happily admitted to being a huge Polanski fan and to drawing on two Polanski films in particular, *Repulsion* and *The Tenant*, for the kind of atmosphere they were hoping to create in *Barton Fink*. An influence that Joel didn't mention but that critics would notice was Stanley Kubrick's *The Shining*, based on the Stephen King novel. This story of a writer losing his mind in an empty hotel would have more than a little in common with the Coens' film. Perhaps the most quietly frightening moment in *The Shining* occurs when the audience sees what the writer, played by Jack Nicholson, has been typing all these weeks: the same sentence, over and over. The Coens would rewrite this moment by having Barton open the hotel-room Bible and see the opening of his own screenplay printed in it. Other critics would notice debts to David Lynch's *Eraserhead* (for its "liquefaction" according to James Wolcott in *Vanity Fair* — ear pus, oozing walls, a blood-filled bed), to Preston Sturges' *Sullivan's Travels* (for the fast-talking Lipnick and the social-consciousness-versus-Hollywood theme). One astute critic, Philip French of the London *Observer*, even noticed similarities to a film written by Clifford Odets, *Deadline at Dawn*, in which a naïve man wakes up — just like Barton — next to a dead woman that he may or may not have murdered.

Clifford Odets was an American-Jewish playwright, the author of rousing, if now dated, leftist plays *(Waiting for Lefty, Awake and Sing!)* about the dignity and collective power of the poor, who was seduced by the Hollywood offer of big money and unlimited pleasure. The brothers would deliberately echo his style in the few lines that the audience hears of Barton's own play, *Bare Ruined Choirs*, but as usual they were interested only in using Odets as an imaginative starting point. By no means a naïf like Barton, Odets ended up with his own large house, a servant, and many, many women. Barton, on the other hand, would go to Hollywood with the stern hope of keeping to his egocentric principles and beliefs. He would even choose to stay in the decrepit Hotel Earle in order to avoid succumbing to temptation. This casual use of Odets would put the brothers in hot water again with the critics; Ethan would say defensively that Barton was "written as a naïve character [but] that's not to say every left-wing, idealistic person in the world is likewise."

In similar fashion, the brothers would call on the ghost of another actual writer who went to Hollywood, William Faulkner, for the character of W.P. Mayhew. The brothers would put an odd twist in the character, however, by making him a fraud; it is his secretary, Audrey, who has written his last books. That revelation might play to some of the movie's themes, such as the ambiguous nature of authenticity and artistic sincerity, but again some literal-minded critics would take offense at the way the brothers played fast and loose with the details of Faulkner's life.

Just as a screenplay by Odets probably influenced Joel and Ethan, so may have one by Faulkner. When Barton is given the assignment of writing a Wallace Beery wrestling picture for Capitol Pictures ("Big men in tights!" shouts Geisler. "You know the drill!"), the joke is that no such Hollywood genre actually existed. But in fact Faulkner worked, without credit, on a Wallace Beery picture about wrestling called *Flesh*, which was released in 1932. The brothers claimed not to have known about the movie until after they had written theirs, but that was probably a playful red herring. It is hard to believe that they did not come across a reference to it when reading about writers in Hollywood.

John Goodman's character, on the other hand, was a totally fictional creation. The boys gave him an all-American first name, Charlie, and a comfortingly pastoral last one, Meadows — at least as the name he would call himself. In fact, his real name was the harsh German "Karl Mundt," and he would turn out to be a notoriously sadistic serial killer. (Later the brothers, always the kidders, would credit the "Newsreel Announcer" on *The Hudsucker*

Joel and Ethan look over the *Barton Fink* script, which took them just three weeks to write   EVERETT COLLECTION

Proxy as "Karl Mundt.") Why a German name? Mostly because the brothers had decided to set the film in 1941, the year of the American entry into World War II, and making this embodiment of evil a German seemed like an interesting idea. Like some of their other ideas, the brothers didn't find it necessary to push this one too far in their own minds, aside from carrying out the metaphor (if that's what it was) by giving the two detectives in the story representative Axis names as well (Mastrionetti and Deutsch). It was simply a kind of game-playing around the central idea of an unlikely, needful, and possibly dangerous friendship between two men.

In the past, Joel and Ethan had relied on genres to help structure their films. *Blood Simple* was revisionist film noir, *Raising Arizona* a screwball comedy crossed with a Warner Brothers cartoon, *Miller's Crossing* a rewrite of Dashiell Hammett and gangster pictures. But *Barton Fink* was only a Hollywood satire in passing, and the brothers knew they were on less familiar ground — that neither they nor their audiences could rely on their assumptions about any film genre to help them through. "We tried something different," Ethan said. "It's a boring comedy. It definitely is slow-paced. It is sort of confused, generically." Before starting to write they had a sense of the story's trajectory and knew that at a point about halfway through it would suddenly change or "turn," as they liked to put it. It would be the moment when Barton, turning over in bed towards the woman he has just spent the night with, discovers that Audrey is dead. Without question, this image — an ocean of blood staining the bed — has elements of the horror genre, as would other aspects of the film to follow, but it was not a horror film either. If anything this turning was bound to disturb and worry audiences even more.

The brothers' writing method was to talk about each scene before starting to write. Usually it took them four months to write a screenplay (*Miller's Crossing* took nine), but this one seemed to appear almost whole to them. For the other films writing was like leaving for a journey without knowing where they would end up; this time they knew the ending before starting. Various suggestive symbols — not just the names but such things as the picture on Barton's wall of the girl on the beach, came to them in a rush. Explaining their elusiveness, Joel said, "Most of those things, they're supposed to be evocative rather than symbols of hidden meaning. I like the idea of the woman in the picture. In a weird kind of way it's emotional, evocative, rather than having a specific kind of meaning."

Barton Fink would become the brothers' most analyzed film as critics and students worked to uncover meaning, but Joel and Ethan themselves felt that aspects of what they wrote were "indecipherable." Of course, it is also true that what may be indecipherable for an author (because it is based in the subconscious) can sometimes be discerned by others.

The screenplay opens with Barton backstage, listening to the actors performing the last lines of his play, *Bare Ruined Choirs*. Interestingly, the brothers would later decide to have one of the voices of the actors be John Turturro's, giving a strangely eerie quality to the opening, as if Barton were projecting himself onstage. The play is a critical smash and in a bar afterwards Barton's agent tells him that Capitol Pictures wants him to come to Hollywood and write for the movies at a thousand dollars a week. But Barton — who shows himself to be humorless and pretentious — resists, declaring that he and others are on the verge of creating "a new, living theater of and about and for the common man!"

Nevertheless, Barton goes; in the next scene he is checking into the lugubrious Hotel Earle. His room, where so much of the film is set, is described in the script as "small and cheaply furnished," with a "lumpy bed," a table for his typewriter, and a picture on the wall of a "bathing beauty" shielding her eyes as she sits on the beach gazing at the ocean. In bed, Barton is tormented by a mosquito. In the morning is his first meeting with Jack Lipnick, head of Capitol Pictures. The brothers have great fun giving Lipnick speeches that parody the Hollywood moguls. "We're only interested in one thing: Can you tell a story, Bart? Can you make us laugh, can you make us cry, can you make us wanna break out in joyous song? Is that more than one thing?"

Barton, overwhelmed, is assigned a wrestling picture for Wallace Beery, but back in his hotel room he manages only to write the opening fade-in before coming down with writer's block. A complaint to the front desk about noise from the next room results in his meeting with Charlie Meadows, a seemingly decent insurance salesman who both sympathizes with and admires Barton and his ambitions. "Strange as it may seem, Charlie," says Barton, "I guess I write about people like you. The average working stiff. The common man." But Barton is too self-involved and egotistical to listen to any of the stories that Charlie offers to tell him; in the fashion of an ancient Greek play it is this hubris that is Barton's downfall.

Barton also meets the producer of his movie, the fast-talking, aggressive but fearful Ben Geisler, who tells Barton that if he's having trouble writing he should talk to another writer. That sends Barton to W.P. Mayhew, the great southern novelist turned Hollywood hack — a living example of the destructive power of Hollywood for the artist. Meanwhile, Barton is still unable to write and spends his time watching the paste ooze from under the wallpaper as it peels off his wall. Charlie Meadows visits again, and once more Barton fails to hear him, telling Charlie that he envies him for the simplicity of his routine. Barton, on the other hand, has to "plumb the depths" of his own soul every day. Charlie tries to help Barton out of his writer's block by showing him some wrestling moves, a moment in which the brothers may be comically evoking the famous wrestling scene in the film of D.H. Lawrence's novel *Women in Love* and its homosexual undercurrent.

Barton visits W.P. Mayhew again, and finds himself condemning the great writer's drunkenness. He also develops a crush on Mayhew's assistant, Audrey, who tries without success to teach Barton that "Empathy requires . . . understanding." Charlie Meadows disappears on a selling trip, while Barton struggles with his script, finally asking Audrey to come to his hotel room to help him. She stays the night. In the morning he sees a mosquito on her bare back; slapping it, she doesn't move. Blood seeps from beneath her. Barton's screams bring Charlie, who has returned, and who disposes of the body for him.

At Lipnick's pool, Barton has another meeting with the head of Capitol Pictures, who goes down on his knees to kiss Barton's feet. Charlie Meadows, meanwhile, has to go away again, leaving a package for Barton to keep for him. Immediately afterwards Barton is visited by two detectives who reveal that Charlie is really Karl Mundt, a notorious serial killer who likes to decapitate people.

Since Audrey's death Barton has appeared increasingly unstrung. But now, with the knowledge that his only friend in Hollywood is a murderer, he returns to his room. And with the package left by Charlie beside him — we can't help wondering what's in it: Audrey's head? — he begins to type. In a long, intense creative rush he finishes the screenplay, afterwards dancing wildly at a USO dance to celebrate. But when W.P. Mayhew's headless body is found the detectives return to arrest Barton in his room, handcuffing him to the bed. The room starts to get hot and the detectives go out into the hall in time to see the elevator man stumble out of the elevator, his hands pressed to his head. In the screenplay the man falls forward and his head "separates from his neck, hits the floor, and rolls away from his body with a dull irregular trundle sound" — a gruesome but perhaps too ridiculous effect, left out of the final film. Charlie Meadows, AKA Karl Mundt, appears out of the burning elevator with a shotgun and kills one detective, screaming, "I'll show you the life of the mind!" He dispatches the other with a quiet "Heil Hitler."

In Barton's room, Charlie answers Barton's question of "Why me?" with the words "Because you don't listen!" Then he frees Barton, implies that he has murdered Barton's family back in Brooklyn, and goes into his own room, presumably to kill himself.

Barton walks out of the hotel with his finished screenplay and the package Charlie gave him. In Lipnick's office, he finds the studio executive in an officer's uniform. Lipnick informs Barton that his script stinks but refuses to let him out of his contract. In the final scene Barton is walking on a beach, Charlie's package under his arm. He sees a woman on the sand — the same bathing beauty that is in the picture in his hotel room, in the exact same pose. They exchange a few words. She looks out to the ocean. The sun sparkles on the water. The screenplay ends.

In three weeks the first draft was done and the brothers went back to writing *Miller's Crossing*. They showed the draft to John Turturro, who had an unusual opportunity as an actor to give early input to a script. Turturro read books on Clifford Odets and also Michael Gold's novel about immigrant poverty on the Lower East Side, *Jews Without Money*, to better understand the conditions that gave rise to social-activist Jewish artists like Barton. Perhaps because of this research, Turturro seemed to have a more benign and understanding attitude towards his character than the harsh script might invite. For example, he believed that the film script Barton finally writes, which we never get to see, is good, suggesting that the character was able to learn something of value. In preparation, Turturro even learned to type, typing an imaginary letter to Barton's parents that the brothers left on the hotel-room desk during the shoot.

The Writer Is King, but Actors Help

Joel and Ethan took their new script to Twentieth Century Fox, which had already agreed to finance *Miller's Crossing*. But while a gangster picture seemed like it had a reasonable chance at financial success, a film about a self-important blocked writer and a friend who turns out to be a murderer did not sound like blockbuster material to anybody. However, the brothers were keeping the budget to a reasonable $9 million, and besides, they were such a prestige item now that Fox had to fend off other producers. For their money, they received only domestic distribution rights; foreign rights went to the brothers' old supporters at Circle Releasing in the last of their three-picture deal.

While the two stars were already on board, the brothers had to fill in the cast. It wasn't hard to decide on Michael Lerner to play the head of Capitol Pictures ("The writer is king here at Capitol Pictures. You don't believe me, take a look at your paycheck at the end of every week — *that's* what we think of the writer"). A veteran of many theater productions, a character actor in films such as the remake of *The Postman Always Rings Twice*, and a star in miniseries like *Ruby and Oswald*, Lerner had actually played a studio head before — not once, but twice. He had taken on the roles of both Harry Cohn and Jack Warner for television movies. The brothers, who must have had great fun writing the part, had borrowed Harry Cohn's vulgar mouth ("You still think the whole world revolves around whatever rattles inside that little kike head of yours"). They had also taken an incident from Jack Warner's life; when war was declared, Warner called on the wardrobe department to make him an officer's uniform. To prepare for the role, Lerner watched several Preston Sturges movies to help him in his spitfire delivery of his lines.

The brothers had written some smaller, but quite juicy parts, and cast them all well. Tony Shalhoub, known for the television show *Wings* but until now appearing in only a couple of films, would be Ben Geisler, the producer in charge of Barton's wrestling picture. Like Lerner, Shalhoub had the ability to talk very, very fast in a veritable machine-gun spray of words. "The thing that struck me about the script," Shalhoub said, "is that there's a certain desperation in all the characters. [Geisler's] cocky when we first meet him, but he's sweating and his stomach's a mess." John Mahoney, cast as the alcoholic southern writer W.P. Mayhew, was born in England and came to the United States when he was 19. A book editor for many years, Mahoney did not become a professional actor until he was 35. He became known as a member of the Steppenwolf Theater in Chicago, and had moved on to film and television, although he did not yet have the high profile that he would later achieve as the father on *Frasier*. Mahoney too had some insight into the script through the perspective of his character. "Barton is extremely nice, extremely introverted, and doesn't think of very much except himself and his work. And I think that Mayhew humanizes him. He shows Barton that the fact that he is a writer does not mean that he is some sanctified holy person, and that he's a human being and part of the human race, with all its frailties and all its glories." This is nicely put, although whether Barton actually learns this lesson is another question.

The only female role of substance — as Mayhew's assistant, Audrey — went to the fine Australian actress Judy Davis, a woman who could convey sharp wit and intelligence with a single look or word. Lipnick's yes-man, Lou Breeze, a man paid to suffer being humiliated by his boss, was another part written by the brothers for an actor — this time Jon Polito, whom they had cast in *Miller's Crossing*. The actor was flattered. "I was inspired by a sketch [costume designer] Richard Hornung had done of the character," he said of his approach to the small role. "My idea was one of those little papier mâché dolls where you unscrew it, there's another doll inside. Also a sort of bowling pin with glasses."

Joel and Ethan had always been comfortable working with the same technical and creative crew. They might be loyal by nature, but it was also to their advantage to work with people who understood them and their methods. Not everyone liked directors/producers/writers who were as *involved* as the Coens. But the brothers lost their closest collaborator when Barry Sonnenfeld's career took off on its own meteoric rise; now the emotionally sensitive cinematographer was going to direct his own films. His first, *The Addams Family*, to be released in the same year as *Barton Fink*, would be a box-office hit. His follow-up films, *Get Shorty* and the megahit *Men in Black*, would mark him as one of the most financially successful directors in Hollywood. Joel and Ethan must have looked on in appreciative wonder.

However, their immediate problem was finding another cinematographer. The English-born Roger Deakins had begun as a painter before working on documentaries shot under difficult conditions — a yacht race, the war in Rhodesia. In the mid-eighties he worked on his first features, *Another Time, Another Place* and the visually impressive *1984*. Screening his work, the brothers particularly liked his interior shots in *Stormy Monday* and also the look of *Sid and Nancy* and *Pascali's Island*. So they sent Deakins the script.

Deakins, in turn, had just had an unpleasant experience shooting a big,

John Turturro, committed artist, and John Goodman, working stiff
20TH CENTURY FOX/SHOOTING STAR

expensive commercial film called *Air America*. Although his agent presented the Coens' script with advice not to take it, Deakins perked up at the thought of a smaller, more personal project. The brothers and Deakins talked, discovering that, like them, he preferred to shoot with fixed rather than zoom lenses and thought a film should be designed in the shooting rather than the editing room. And he was a hands-on guy who liked to operate his own camera. Signing on, Deakins could not have known that he too was joining the Coens' continuing company of filmmakers.

Although the film would need a few location sites, most of the scenes had to take place in the Hotel Earle. The grandiosely seedy Earle had to be a set, and Dennis Gassner began raising it on a Culver Studios soundstage. This was going to be the first film the brothers actually made in Hollywood. Gassner dubbed the style he created "distressed deco": everything about the set, including the furniture, was built and then severely "aged" to give the hotel a feeling of former elegance now fallen into extreme decay. Barton's room was the most important setting in the film, and not only because it would be used more than any other. Taking even farther the way they used Tom's room in *Miller's Crossing*, the brothers wanted Barton's ever-present and claustrophobic room to be a projection of his mind.

Gassner even designed four different wallpapers: an English William Morris style for the tenement setting of Barton's New York play, a gray damask for the commissary of Capitol Pictures, rotting banana leaves for the hallway of the Hotel Earle, and, most notably, the "bile green" paper of Barton's room. It would be from underneath the latter that a vile ooze would mysteriously appear, causing the paper to curl off the wall. The special-effects crew spent some time perfecting this "goopus," as it was dubbed. As Gassner half joked, "If *Miller's Crossing* was about columns, the theme for *Barton Fink* is wallpaper. This is the wallpaper movie."

The same attention was lavished by Richard Hornung on the costumes. Of Barton's own outfits he said: "We designed him like a dinosaur — totally out of touch with the world, in that it's 1942 and his clothes are much earlier: shoulderless, academic, a little tweed suit that he wears all the time. A lot of the design is based on Barton's will to control. . . . His ties are thirties ties, very early, and they don't even tie by themselves. Like a little boy's tie, with this little fake knot." This old-fashioned style is interesting in light of many critics' remarks that Barton's committed-writer routine rightly belongs to the decade before the one in which the film is set. The brothers were perfectly aware of the incongruity of his type of writer in 1942. Barton was not only out of touch with the people around him; he was out of touch with the decade, a kind of nostalgic dreamer. His shelf of hair and round glasses suggest George S. Kaufman, but the brothers didn't intend any actual reference to the playwright and screenwriter. The hair, which Turturro and the brothers referred to as "the wedge," would grow higher during the course of the shoot. Turturro would later say, "It got to nine centimeters. We had to control it; it was getting out of hand." One or two critics would even suggest that Barton actually looks a little like the Coens themselves. If true, it was a very wry and very strange joke the brothers were playing on themselves.

As for Charlie Meadows, Hornung said "We wanted a real working-class feel: shirt sleeves rolled up and ties, suspenders, and pleated slacks." Hornung gave Charlie a gabardine suit and a hat with a wide band and big crown. His tie, with its mildly pornographic image on the reverse, was his salesman's calling card. In contrast to Barton's buttoned-down need for control, Hornung wanted Charlie to be the living embodiment of chaos.

The other characters received almost equally well-considered treatment. Lipnick was dressed "sort of like an automobile" (Michael Lerner himself found glasses just like those of Jack Warner), while his sidekick, Lou Breeze, lived in "a real lonely suit," and Ben Geisler might have been a "gangster." And just so the significance of detectives Deutsch and Mastrionetti wasn't lost on anyone, Hornung made their suits "a bit of a take-off on the uniforms worn by the Axis powers" — gray with red accents for the German, olive brown for the Italian. Audrey's dresses received a lot of tailoring detail, the overall effect being to give her a film-noir feel.

Ready, Set, Ooze

For the first time since bunking with Sam Raimi, the brothers were encamped in Hollywood, an experience that would itself pay off when they later drew upon their experiences and friendships there to write a very Californian story called *The Big Lebowski*. They began to shoot *Barton Fink* on June 27, 1990, and would finish 45 days later. It was a very controlled shoot. Unlike *Miller's Crossing*, whose story the brothers felt they had less control over than usual and so needed more footage for the editing process, this time they shot only what they needed. Among the locations used were a historic theater called the Orpheum for Barton's Broadway play, the bar of the dry-docked Queen Mary in Long Beach, the Park Plaza Hotel for the USO dance, and the Capitol Pictures men's room. For the long corridor leading up to W.P. Mayhew's bungalow the brothers used the former MGM lot, now Columbia Pictures, while an actual bungalow on the old Zoetrope Studios lot (now Hollywood Center) became Ben Geisler's. On Geisler's wall can be seen a film poster using a shot from a scene in *Miller's Crossing* that didn't make it to final cut; in reverse homage, an apartment house in the gangster picture is called the Barton Arms. Lipnick's pool belonged to a psychiatrist couple; it had once been owned by Gloria Swanson, the star of one of Hollywood's great movies about itself, *Sunset Boulevard*. All Gassner had to do was add the Greek statues. And the final scene, in which Barton walks by the ocean and sees the same woman whose picture has been on his wall all this time (figure out the meaning of that!) was shot near Zuma Beach.

But of course most days were spent on the sets built on the Culver lot, and the preponderance of interior scenes made the shoot feel rather claustrophobic. Tony Shalhoub found that the experience felt much like theater, especially in the way the Coens rehearsed the actors. Certainly the hardest-working actor on the set was John Turturro; all the other characters, including John Goodman's, were easy to find in comparison with Barton Fink. "I know they aren't thought of as actor's directors," said Turturro, "but they've been as good as anyone I've worked with, if not better." The actor tried to see his character as less of a grotesque and more as a person who simply hadn't found his way. "*Barton Fink* is about the journey of a young person trying to establish who he is to himself." He noted that "A great comic performance usually has great pathos and human- ity." Turturro, who himself had written a screenplay, even worked on a script for a wrestling picture called *The Burlyman* in order to feel more like Barton. Even so, Turturro found physical qualities for Barton that made him less than appeal- ing. He swiveled his head "like a yogi"; he made him awkward and stiff; he brought him from moments of almost paralyzed inwardness to extreme hyste- ria. Joel thought the performance brought depths to his and Ethan's creation. "You could describe Barton as a kind of phony writer who comes to L.A., but that wouldn't do justice to the character really, and to what John has done with it. Because he hasn't condescended to the character. You're aware of all the bad parts of Barton, all the things that are not really attractive about him, and John makes them both more horrible and more human at the same time — it makes your feelings about the character weirdly ambivalent. It's definitely a very com- plicated performance."

While Turturro and the others were wrestling with their parts, the technical crew had to make the shots work. Like Sonnenfeld in the last picture, Deakins shot with a shallow focus to give the screen image a center of attention. Lighting effects were used to give a sickly quality to the scenes. For example, the hallway of the hotel was lit only with wall lights, which Deakins had colored yellow. And of course there were two classic Coen brothers shots that were a pain to get right. One begins with the camera on Audrey's feet in Barton's bed, tracks right through the bathroom door, and goes into the sink and down the drain into the pipe. (Judy Davis had left the set by then and the feet of a stand-in — production man- ager Alma Kuttruff — were used.) Appearing as one take, it was actually two,

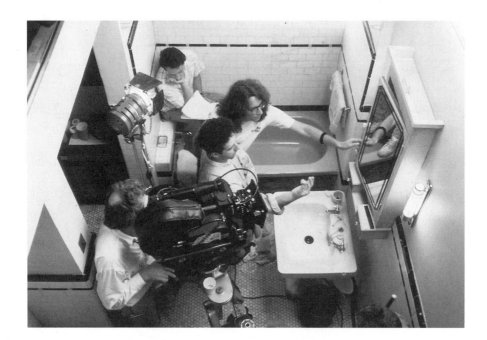

Filming *Barton Fink,* the brothers turn the Hotel Earle setting into a living — if decaying — character

divided when the camera dissolved to black in the drain. A separate shot, using a miniature jib arm and a remote camera, did the second shot down the interior of the pipe. The other, during the USO dance, goes into a musician's trumpet. A remote camera was also used for a shot of Geisler's office, which begins on the typewriter keys of a secretary and then ping-pongs about the room.

Nor did all the "easier" shots always go smoothly. During the shooting of the dance in the Park Plaza Hotel in Los Angeles, the fire sprinklers suddenly went off, soaking the orchestra musicians. Lights couldn't be turned back on until permission came from the fire marshal. Also tricky was getting the "goopus," the slime behind the wallpaper in Barton's room, just right. One stagehand had goopus-administering as his sole responsibility.

As in *Miller's Crossing*, which *Barton Fink* echoes in many ways, the brothers had to shoot a burning sequence. Here it was the Hotel Earle itself, the corridor of which was actually two different sets built in a former seaplane hangar near Long Beach. One set was used for straight scenes, the other for the special effects in the climactic finale, conducted by Robert Spurlock of Stetson Visual Services. It must have been difficult and tense to shoot, as the fire begins with a few flames licking up from the elevator, then spreading across the walls into a full conflagration. The images that Deakins shot — such as Barton's view from his bed of Charlie, framed in the doorway with fire leaping around him — were powerful beyond words. And, with Charlie charging down the hall firing his shotgun and bellowing, the climax became a bizarre and frightening vision of hell.

Cannes and Can Not

For *Barton Fink* the brothers decided not to hire an editor but instead to edit the film themselves under the collective pseudonym of Roderick Jaynes, which they hadn't used since *Blood Simple.* Joel and Ethan even took the joke so far as to let "Jaynes" write the introduction to the published screenplays of *Barton Fink* and *Miller's Crossing* when the two scripts were published, appropriately in a single volume, by the English house Faber and Faber. The Coens liked writing comic and self-deprecating introductions to all their published screenplays, but this one went farthest of all as they let Jaynes, the supposed editor on *Beyond Mombassa* and *Operation Fort Petticoat*, condemn the brothers as amateurs whose scripts were filled with "malformed thoughts." He even claimed that the brothers took *Barton Fink* away from him and gave it to another editor named "Michael Berenbaum" to get more of "the Hebrew point of view."

Because the shooting followed the screenplay even more strictly than usual, the editing was a fairly straightforward process. Their composer, Carter Burwell, who was now writing music for other films as well (*Psycho III*, *Doc Hollywood*), created a very minimalist score that was in marked contrast to the lyrical richness of the music for *Miller's Crossing*. "We discovered," said Burwell, "that the more somber and withheld the score was, the more hilarious the movie became." Perhaps few viewers would find the movie hilarious, but the score was indeed effective, especially in the way that it meshed closely with the important and creepy sound effects like the incessantly buzzing mosquito in Barton's room. During the scene where Barton finally starts writing his screenplay, Burwell used the rhythm of the typewriter to jive with percussion instruments in order to "get a little bit of a groove going." Elsewhere the score was more "tentative," as the composer put it, to emphasize the uneasy tone of the film.

When Joel and Ethan had begun as filmmakers, film festivals had been an important way to get first reviews, audience feedback, and introductions to distributors. They might be famous now, at least among the art-house crowd, but festivals could still be useful in boosting a film's profile and prestige. That certainly happened when *Barton Fink* was accepted for official competition at the 1991 Cannes Film Festival, the most high-profile and prestigious of all. By an extraordinary coincidence, the jury that year was headed by none other than Roman Polanski, a director whom the brothers not only admired but whose work had particularly influenced *Barton Fink*. Raised in Poland, Polanski was a young boy when the Nazis sent his parents to a concentration camp. His mother died there and her son was shunted from one family to another, an experience that left him with a permanently dark and uneasy outlook. "Roman Polanski is a favorite," Joel once said. "He's terrific. *Knife in the Water*, *Repulsion*, *The Tenant*, *Chinatown*, *Rosemary's Baby* — I love them all." Polanski pretty much controlled the jury, since he had agreed to head it on the condition that he could choose the other members himself.

The result was that the film won an unprecedented three awards — the Palme d'Or for best film, as well as the Best Director (Joel Coen) and Best Actor (John Turturro) awards. Some journalists were a touch cynical about the hat

Joel holds the brothers' Palme d'Or for *Barton Fink*
ARCHIVE PHOTOS

trick. By awarding a film that showed his own influence, wasn't Polanski merely honoring himself? On the other hand, the film was directed with style and assurance, Turturro's performance was astonishingly risky, and whether or not one liked the film, it would be hard to deny that it was creepily fascinating and brimming with suggestive ideas about the nature of art and the self.

American distributors knew that awards from Cannes did not ensure large audiences in Ohio. In fact, sometimes Americans were wary of European award-winners, expecting them to be obscure and pretentious. And the truth was, with *Miller's Crossing* having failed at the box office, it was hardly likely that *Barton Fink* would set any records. But good reviews in the right publications could ensure a steady art-house following and maybe more.

Not surprisingly, though, the critics found the brothers' most puzzling and elusive film — well, puzzling and elusive. Yes, its Hollywood parody was funny. Yes, its horror elements did make one squirm in one's seat. Yes, it was original. But what *was* the lesson that Barton learned? What was inside the box that Charlie Meadows gave him? Even those who strongly admired the film had a hard time conveying that admiration in a way that would bring in audiences. David Ansen of *Newsweek* called it "a nightmare dressed in the bold outlines of a cartoon . . . a post-modernist Faustian comedy whose ultimate destination is hell itself. Creepily original, acted with relish, *Barton Fink* is a savagely original work. It lodges in your head like a hatchet." A hatchet in the head? Just what the average moviegoer is looking for.

In like fashion, Dave Kehr of the *Chicago Tribune* called the film a "strange, funny, and furiously inventive comedy [that] puts the Coen brothers in a whole new league. . . . They've redeemed the emptiness that haunted their early work by taking emptiness itself as a subject — the ultimate postmodern gesture." In *Rolling Stone* Peter Travers praised the film highly but admitted that it was "Sometimes enigmatic to the point of exasperation. . . ." He warned viewers that if they did not meet the Coens "halfway" seeing the film would be "an empty exercise that will bore you breathless." But if you did, he said, you would find "a comic nightmare that will stir your imagination like no film in years." Brian D. Johnson of *Maclean's* also liked the film but had to note that it was "not for all tastes."

On the other hand, those critics who did not like the film had far less trouble numbering their reasons. Terrence Rafferty of the *New Yorker*, who had already dissed *Miller's Crossing*, read the film's postmodern qualities in a far less positive way than had the critic of the *Chicago Tribune*. The film, Rafferty wrote, "is densely packed with allusions, clever dialogue, ingenious visual jokes, startling plot twists, and imaginative atmospheric effects, yet it feels thin. It's an empty tour de force, and what's dismaying about the picture is that the filmmakers . . . seem inordinately pleased with its hermetic meaninglessness." Rafferty would strike a note with other critics by claiming that the brothers, previously more light-hearted in their approach, were now trying to be intellectuals and artists. Instead, he insists, they are merely "nihilist showoffs." He took exception to their misuse of Clifford Odets, who "wasn't a phony, or a buffoon, or a talentless hack," and to the way the filmmakers set Barton up only to "invent torments" for him. He also attacked John Turturro's performance: "His Barton Fink is the most fanatically detailed caricature of a nerd since the heyday of Jerry Lewis. . . ."

Although Rafferty wasn't explicit, his attack on the film — whose formal qualities he admitted to admiring at least somewhat — was ultimately a moral one. Paradoxically it is both the cynical message, as these critics perceived it, and at the same time the emptiness or lack of message that they condemned. One critic, Jonathan Rosenbaum of the Chicago *Reader*, claimed that the film was sending out the following lessons: "Socially committed artists are frauds"; "Genuine artists like William Faulkner are frauds too"; "Hollywood producers are frauds"; "The very notion of the common man is fraudulent. . . ."

In part it was the critical historical period that the brothers chose to set their film in that set the critics off. The *Village Voice*'s J. Hoberman's moral condemnation was centered on the film's depiction of Jews. "At the period when *Barton Fink* is set, the virtual acme of worldwide anti-Semitism, America's two most potent Jewish stereotypes were the vulgar Hollywood mogul and the idealistic New York communist. . . . *Barton Fink* locks these stereotypes in a sadomasochistic embrace. . . ."

Among all the reviews of *Miller's Crossing*, the *Voice* was virtually the only publication to take exception to the portrait of Bernie Bernbaum. Part of the reason was that the role was relatively small, and even critics who noted the brothers' riff on an old stereotype might have preferred not to deal with it. After all, the Coens *were* Jewish. This time, however, the Jewish question was much harder to ignore. James Wolcott in *Vanity Fair* also took it up. "What makes the movie such an audacious sickie is that the Coen brothers — themselves Jewish — never attempt to make us identify with Barton's plight. They keep him and his attitudes in a jar." Yet unlike Hoberman, Wolcott didn't simply condemn the brothers or want to label them self-hating Jews. "I never felt watching the movie that the Coen brothers were indulging in something as obvious and personal as Jewish self-hatred. The movie has too much conscious effrontery. . . . It satirizes the Jewish sense of victimization, without denying that victimization exists."

In reacting less emotionally, Wolcott was able to see farther into the film. The portrait of Jews in *Barton Fink* wasn't personal. An astute observer of the brothers' films would see that Joel and Ethan had always used types as the basis for their characters. The hot-blooded Texans in *Blood Simple*, the simple-minded white trash of *Raising Arizona*, the hard-boiled gangsters of *Miller's Crossing* — all of them were based on existing portraits from film and books rather than life. A few years later nearly everyone would like the film *Fargo* with its quaint-talking Minnesotan characters; only people actually *from* Minnesota would take offense at what they perceived as being stereotyped as good-natured dummies. What none of the critics of *Barton Fink* wrote about was what exactly was the *effect* of basing characters on such types. Without question the portrayal of Jews in *Barton Fink* deserved close scrutiny; but to simply condemn them was to close one's mind to what Joel and Ethan were doing, whether consciously or not.

The complaints about the film made the brothers uncharacteristically defensive during the promotional tour. Asked by the *Village Voice* about whether words like "kike" might offend some viewers, the brothers at first acted as if they didn't understand. Finally Joel said with a laugh, "Are you saying, are we worried about people thinking we painted a broad ethnic stereotype and taking offense at that? . . . No, I'm not worried about that, I know it will happen." Remembering that the *Voice* has been the most outspoken critic of their Jewish characters, Joel and Ethan became awkward and silent, seeming to lose their cool for a moment. Then they struggled to differentiate between creating an unpleasant character, which they asserted was not anti-Semitic, and making a film that said, for example, Jews control Hollywood, which they agreed would be.

If that wasn't enough, they also had to answer to charges that the film was too slow and enigmatic. Ethan said, "I think the movie's really entertaining. We tried to make it that way." Laughing, he added, "Was there any whining there?" Joel also defended it. "I . . . don't think it's as difficult as some people think it is. I mean, some people come out going, 'I don't get it.' And I don't know what they're trying to 'get,' what they're struggling for."

This last statement of Joel's is illuminating. The simple truth is that people naturally *do* want meaning, they want signs and references and symbols to actually point to something. In the same way, they expect a movie set in a historical period to have something to say about that period. Why, for example, does the hotel conflagration at the end of *Barton Fink* echo the fate of the Jews in the Holocaust? What, as some critics asked, is gained by the reference? Perhaps Joel and Ethan confounded people with their playfulness, their tendency to throw in an idea or image, to use a period or a character type without wanting to take the implications any further. For the Coens, making films was a game unto itself, with its own internal rules. It wasn't supposed to relate to the outside world, to tell us something about "reality." In fact, that may have been the real lesson for Barton, the misguided artist who thought his words could make a difference. Film isn't life, Joel and Ethan might have been saying. It might borrow from life, but that's not the same thing. It's just film. And why should it be anything else?

CHAPTER SEVEN

THE COMEDY OF BUSINESS

THE HUDSUCKER PROXY

"Norville, you can't trust people here like you did in Muncie . . ."
— Amy in *The Hudsucker Proxy*

With such vehement disagreement as to its meaning and value, *Barton Fink* ought to have been the subject of heated debate if nothing else. But aside from the dueling critics, it wasn't. Despite some awards and nominations (New York Film Critics Awards for Cinematography and Best Supporting Actress, three Academy Award nominations), the film generated little business. Whether this was proof of American audiences' dislike for difficult or "cold" films or simply their anti-intellectualism, it must have been disappointing to the brothers after the failure of *Miller's Crossing*. *Raising Arizona* had seemed to show that there *was* an audience for Coen brothers films, but perhaps that film was just the exception that proved the rule. No wonder the brothers decided to get away for a while after the opening of *Barton Fink*. Together they traveled to Nepal in November of 1991. They traveled from Katmandu by bus to the Langtang Valley and then on foot with some hired Sherpas into the Himalayas. It was surprisingly cold and they both suffered from altitude sickness.

Back in New York, Joel and Ethan returned to work. Since *Blood Simple* they had always been working on one picture or another, and although their films were tanking at the box office their critical reputation was still high. (Those Cannes awards didn't hurt.) But to immediately do another small film like *Barton Fink* must not have seemed like the right move. Besides, the brothers never liked to repeat themselves; they thrived on novelty and change.

They could write a new screenplay, but they already had at least a couple of unproduced scripts still lying around. One they had never lost interest in was the film they had written with their old buddy Sam Raimi, *The Hudsucker Proxy*. Until now they hadn't had the clout to raise the large budget the film would need. Nor perhaps, had they felt quite ready to tackle its technical complexities. But now felt like the right time, at least in part because it seemed to Joel and Ethan that more people might actually *like* the movie. Later Joel would say — wrongly, as it turned out — "Nobody will be scratching their heads in this one, wondering, 'What the hell. . . .' It's a comedy." And also: "*Barton Fink* was never intended to be a movie that would play in malls in middle America. Whereas *Hudsucker* is a more mainstream movie, in terms of its ambitions." And Ethan would say, "It is sort of a sweet movie. For that matter, *Raising Arizona* was a sort of sweet-natured movie. Also the last movie we made that made any significant amount of money." In other words, the brothers were under the impression that, unlike their dark, cynical, ironic films of the very recent past, this one had the potential for broad appeal — just like the 1930s comedies that had inspired it.

Joel and Ethan and Sam Raimi had written the script back in 1984, when the three of them, along with Frances McDormand, were sharing an apartment in Los Angeles during their first stay there. The brothers in particular were big fans of the films of Preston Sturges — *The Great McGinty, The Lady Eve, The Palm Beach Story*, and especially the Hollywood satire *Sullivan's Travels*. Like the brothers, Sturges wrote his own witty, talk-filled screenplays, created eccentric characters, liked to use a recurring company of actors, had a strong visual sense, and made films that were more ironic and satirical than other American directors. The following description of Sturges' work, from *The Oxford Companion to Film*, might just as well fit the brothers: "His view of the world and his fellow men seemed to be sour and often contemptuous, but the characters are usually presented with a certain affection and this, together with the pervading humor, gives the films a rather ambiguous tone."

The brothers were thinking of other writers and directors from the period as well: Howard Hawks *(His Girl Friday)*, who also liked fast and funny dialogue; and the more sentimental Frank Capra, with his tales *(Meet John Doe, Mr. Smith Goes to Washington, It's a Wonderful Life)* of decent and ordinary men forced into heroic roles. These movies made use of actors — Gary Cooper, Henry Fonda, Jimmy Stewart, Cary Grant, Barbara Stanwyck, Katharine Hepburn, Rosalind Russell — of incomparable appeal who made audiences identify with and love them. Their depression and wartime audiences would come out of the cinema feeling a little better about the world and their lives in it.

The brothers did not want to make a parody of such films; they had no desire to deride them. As Ethan said, "It's the case where, having seen those movies, we say, 'They're really fun — let's do one,' as opposed to, 'They're really fun — let's comment upon them.'" And so they paced around the apartment and wrote, taking turns at the typewriter. Whenever they got stuck Raimi would try different tricks to get the boys started again. He'd move objects in the room around so that when Ethan paced he'd be thrown off, and he even claimed to have thrown firecrackers at them. Raimi called the script a "big-business comedy. It's a return to the very large love-story comedies they used to make in the forties and early fifties." Accounts of the writing make it sound as if Raimi took a backseat to Joel and Ethan. He would suggest an idea and they would laugh at it; for example, he wanted Sidney J. Mussburger to turn out to be a nice guy who had gone down the wrong path. Joel and Ethan said no — they wanted a film without shadings, with only good guys and bad guys.

The first image the brothers had was of their hero, who they named Norville Barnes, about to jump from the window of a skyscraper. They worked from there, trying to figure out how he got there and how they could save him. What they came up with was the story of a small-town boy, a dreamer, and his rise to the top of a malevolent corporation. The setting was the fifties, although once again the brothers had no special interest in the period or concern for accuracy, and the film would end up drawing on the art-deco style of the thirties and forties for costumes, furniture, and set design. To frame the picture they used a narrator once more — this time not a main character as in *Raising Arizona,* but a sort of stock figure from earlier films, the wise black man watching the foolishness of white folk. They named him Moses and gave him the job of keeper of the skyscraper clock. They made Norville a true innocent, a hick coming to the big city in the hope of making his fortune, who gets taken advantage of by those more sophisticated and cynical than him. And of course there was a female interest, a reporter who, in Hollywood tradition, was quick-thinking and hard-nosed but also, at heart, womanly. The scenes with her at the newspaper allowed for the kind of breakneck banter worthy of the screenplays of Ben Hecht. "We were having fun," Ethan remembered of those writing days. "The script, which contains a lot of traditional genre elements, was marked by a kind of heartwarming fantasy element out of Frank Capra. It also had a lot of verbal comedy, the kind you see in films by Preston Sturges or Howard Hawks, with dialogue delivered in a rapid-fire, machine-gun style. But it was bigger and broader, with physical comedy sequences and a lot of oddball action."

It was easy enough to see the influences on the characters. Norville was the Jimmy Stewart character, Amy Archer (the woman reporter sent out to cover Norville's rise to the presidency of Hudsucker Industries) the Katharine Hepburn or Rosalind Russell role, and Mussburger was the traditional Edward Arnold, the evil and greedy capitalist. The only trouble was finding an ending — some way to save Norville as he jumps in despair from the skyscraper, a setting which was as central to the film as Barton's hotel room was in *Barton Fink*. Back in 1984 the three friends left it unfinished, but now they picked it up again, dusted it off, and gave it a deus ex machina ending to save Norville from his plunge off the Hudsucker building.

The screenplay begins with the voice of Moses ("It's 1958 — anyway, for a few mo' minutes it is") telling us that while New York is about to celebrate New Year's, Norville Barnes, president of Hudsucker Industries, is crawling out his office window and onto the ledge. How did he get to this desperate state? Moses takes us back to the arrival in the city of Norville, a graduate of the Muncie College of Business Administration but with no experience to get a job. Meanwhile, high up in the offices of Hudsucker Industries, President Waring Hudsucker runs down the long boardroom table during a meeting and crashes through the window to his death. Hudsucker's shares will soon become available to the public; what are the board members to do? One, the evil Sid Mussburger, immediately gets an idea. The board must hire a proxy — "Some jerk we can really push around" — whose presence causes the stock price to fall dramatically so that the board members can buy it up.

Norville gets a job in the madhouse mailroom of Hudsucker Industries, but he already has an idea, which he shows to a fellow worker as a crude circle drawn on a piece of paper. "You know, for kids!" When he is sent upstairs with an urgent "blue letter," Norville meets Sid Mussburger and shows him his idea, proving to Mussburger that he is the perfect sap for the job as president. As the plan begins to work and the stock to fall, the editor of the *Manhattan Argus* challenges his reporters to get the real scoop on Norville. Pulitzer Prize winner Amy Archer takes up the challenge, easily fooling the naïve Norville by sidling up to him in a coffee shop and pretending to need a job — a scene made particularly funny by the running commentary of two coffee-shop veterans in the sort of dialogue exchange that frequently enlivens the script. Using a false name, Amy becomes his secretary, meanwhile writing a front-page article about Hudsucker Industries being run by an "Imbecile." Norville gets a prototype of his great idea made — it turns out to be a hula hoop — and the snickering Mussburger puts it into production, thinking it will be a bust. And at first it is, until a toy-store owner throws one out his back door in disgust, and the hoop rolls down the street, to be found by a young boy. He begins to twirl it around his hips and when a screaming pack of children see him, they rush madly towards the toy store. As a movie newsreel informs us, the hula hoop is a smash hit and Norville Barnes is bringing in "untold profits" for the company.

Unfortunately, the success goes to Norville's head — he begins hanging about with "high-fashion model" Za Za, smoking cigars, and living high. And when sales start to slow, Norville approves of layoffs, to the disgust of the formerly smitten Amy, and refuses a new idea from the elevator operator (bendable straws), firing him. The operator goes to the newspaper, claiming that Norville has stolen his ideas. Under attack and having discovered that Amy has lied about her identity, Norville begins drinking on New Year's Eve. He is chased by an angry crowd led by the elevator operator, and takes refuge in the Hudsucker building, where he makes his way up to that fateful ledge where we first met him.

Norville jumps, but before he hits the ground old Moses, keeper of the Hudsucker clock, jams the clock's gears and stops time — "Have you got a better idea?" he asks the audience. While Norville is suspended in midair, the angel of Waring Hudsucker descends and tells Norville to open the blue letter that he never delivered. It turns out that Hudsucker's last letter bequeaths his stock to whoever succeeds him as president, which means Norville. The clock starts again, Norville lands safely on the ground, Amy and Norville reunite, and Norville invents the Frisbee.

Now the brothers had a script they hoped would bring in an audience. All they needed was 25 or 30 million dollars to make it — twice as much as their highest budget to date and three times that of their last film. After the failure of *Barton Fink* they didn't think they had a hope of making it, but the brothers took the script to their agent, Jim Berkus of United Talent Agency, who suggested they see if Joel Silver wanted to produce it. The Coens literally laughed in their agent's face.

Joel Silver? Producer of big-budget action flicks like *48 Hours, Die Hard, Predator, Lethal Weapon,* and their sequels? In total, Silver's films — produced by his own production company, Silver Pictures, which he ran out of a bungalow on the Warner Brothers lot — had grossed $2 billion, making the box office of the Coens' pictures look like they were selling lemonade at two cents a cup. But Joel and Ethan agreed, Silver read the script, and they all had a meeting. The brothers discovered that the producer's reputation for being a silver-tongued, nonstop talker was well deserved. Ethan recounted, "You can't object to being yammered at incessantly by somebody who's really a good talker." For his part, Silver liked the idea of working with real artists. He saw two talented filmmakers who wanted to make a big-budget movie and had finally come around to the idea that maybe it would be nice if more than 12 people saw one of their films. Joel noted, "He said we were morons for shelving it."

"We approached [the partnership with Silver] with a certain trepidation," Joel admitted. "[Silver] is legendary for being a difficult personality, but we didn't see any of that. You hear all this stuff about him, but from our point of view he did exactly what he said he was going to do." That meant not interfering in the making of the film, despite the large amount of money invested. In the end, Silver's only real interference was to convince the brothers not to shoot the film in black and white; he threatened to colorize it if they did.

Silver took the project to Warner Brothers, pitching it something like this: Joel and Ethan Coen made movies that the critics loved but that nobody went to see. He, Joel Silver, made movies the critics hated but that everybody went to see. Here

Tim Robbins, good guy, and Paul Newman, bad guy, in *The Hudsucker Proxy* PHOTOFEST

was a chance for Warner Brothers to have a movie that the critics liked *and* everybody wanted to see. The studio liked the idea, but only if the picture had stars with some box-office magnetism. In the past, Joel and Ethan might have told a studio making such a request to take a hike, but this time they said yes. As Jim Jacks, the executive producer on *Raising Arizona*, explained at the time of the release of *The Hudsucker Proxy:* "[Joel and Ethan will] always try to make a movie as commercial as it has to be to recoup its investment, which is making them nervous. They've never made a movie so expensive that they had to make it *that* commercial, until now." And so the brothers had to go looking for stars.

Instead of just choosing who they wanted, they had to sit down with Silver first. Fortunately, they all found it easy to agree. For Norville Barnes they wanted lanky Tim Robbins, an actor with a farmboy's innocence and natural charm. At the time Robbins was riding high, having just starred in Robert Altman's *The Player* as well as in *Bob Roberts*, a political satire that he had also written and directed. His list of films was impressive, but he was probably best liked by audiences for his performance as the dumb but talented baseball player in *Bull*

Durham. Having played some less than decent guys in his last two pictures, Robbins was pleased to take on Norville. "I jumped at the chance to do a guy who isn't an evil son-of-a-bitch," he said, "a guy who had heart. And Norville's not dumb — he's just ill-equipped to get by in a fiercely competitive world."

An even bigger draw, especially for older audiences, was Paul Newman, whom the brothers chose to play the evil Sid Mussburger. Playing a bad guy was hardly a risk for such a loved and established actor in the later years of his career. Winner of an Academy Award in 1986 for *The Color of Money,* Newman had starred in many great films, including *Cool Hand Luke* and *Butch Cassidy and the Sundance Kid.* Married to Joanne Woodward, he had been honored not only for his work but also for his charity fundraising efforts. Newman, who liked the part, decided not to play Mussburger as a villain, or at least not to think of him that way. "Every character every actor plays has to be the hero," he said.

The next most important actor was certainly the female lead of Amy Archer. Smart-mouthed, quicker on the uptake than the male hacks in the newsroom around her, Amy had to be both sharp and sympathetic so that the audience would want Norville to fall for her. Here the brothers made a slightly risky choice in Jennifer Jason Leigh. Certainly she was a fine actress who had done outstanding work in *Miami Blues* and *Last Exit to Brooklyn.* But she was also peculiar in her mannerisms and not the sort to appeal to every viewer. Leigh prepared for the part by reading biographies of the great leading ladies of the thirties and forties — Jean Arthur, Rosalind Russell, Katharine Hepburn.

Some fine and recognizable actors were chosen for smaller roles as well — Charles Durning as Waring Hudsucker, who crashes through the skyscraper window early in the picture, John Mahoney as the newsroom chief, Peter Gallagher as a lounge singer. Some Coen brothers veterans also got small parts: Steve Buscemi, Jon Polito, Bruce Campbell (from *The Evil Dead*). Warner Brothers voiced their satisfaction at the choice of stars and agreed to back the picture along with PolyGram, the two companies each putting up half the budget with Warner getting domestic distribution rights and PolyGram getting foreign. Warner also brought into the deal Working Title Films, the company that had hit it big with *Four Weddings and a Funeral.* Run by Tim Bevan and Eric Fellner, Working Title was one of Britain's most successful independent production companies. Bevan had started out by producing *My Beautiful Laundrette,* Fellner with *Sid and Nancy,* so it is easy to see why a film by the

Coen brothers would have appealed to them. In fact, they had met the brothers through Frances McDormand, who had a part in their spy thriller *Hidden Agenda*. As promised, though, Joel Silver protected Joel and Ethan's autonomy. The contract gave Warner Brothers the right only to make *suggestions* for editing the film. The brothers still had the final cut.

It wasn't originally the desire for star actors that necessitated the large budget, but the sets that the brothers wanted to build, and with the contract signed the special-effects and building crews were hired on. Indeed, although the brothers had written a thirties-style comic screenplay, their real interest in the project was in building an idealized city of skyscrapers and the visual camera effects they could create with it. It is very telling that before starting to work they screened the science fiction film *Blade Runner*, whose most notable feature was an extraordinary cityscape of the future. The script was really nothing more than a reason to populate the set. In fact, despite the supposedly large size and scope of the movie, it was not that much larger in conception than the Coens' other films. Instead of the Hotel Earle, the dominant setting was the Hudsucker building. *Miller's Crossing* and the film that would come next, *Fargo*, had more locations. The real difference was simply how much that setting cost to build.

The brothers brought in their usual crew — Dennis Gassner for the all-important production design, Richard Hornung for costumes, and Roger Deakins, for his second Coen brothers film, as cinematographer. What the film needed was a 1950s New York City skyline. Joel and Ethan didn't want to use the real New York; too many modern buildings had gone up and, besides, it didn't match the idealized cityscape that they imagined. And so 27 craftsmen working for Stetson Visual Services, under the supervision of Michael McAlister, who had done the effects for *Barton Fink* and knew Gassner from his Zoetrope days, spent three months building. McAlister found that the brothers, unlike many directors he had worked for, already had a clear vision of what they wanted. His job was to match that vision and help put it on celluloid. The crews raised 14 skyscrapers built to a scale of 1/24; each was based on a real New York skyscraper, put side by side to create, as McAlister called it, "a fantasy vision of New York." A separate soundstage was needed to shoot them.

Three separate crews worked on the buildings. One, under chief model-maker Ian Hunter, built the scale miniatures that would be used for the opening fly-through sequence and the falls from the Hudsucker building. These buildings were all based on photographs from a book Gassner had found called *New York in the Forties.* Gassner's own model for the monumental scale of the picture was *Citizen Kane.* Based on the photos, draftsmen drew blueprints and then made simple mock-ups to see how the buildings would look in relation to one another. A camera shot film around the mock-ups to get a better sense of how much detail would be needed. Then the real models were built, the tallest about 20 feet high, and all just two-sided since their backs would not be seen by the camera. A total of 12,000 tiny windows were put in by hand, while a "detail" crew added the cornices and other decoration and also "aged" the buildings to make them look more real. Many of the windows had curtains and other details added behind them.

The Hudsucker building itself, headquarters of the corporation that Norville would become president of, and from whose window he would eventually jump, was the star attraction among the buildings. This was a true fantasy building, a stylistic borrowing from the Woolworth Building in New York, the former Standard Oil Building in Chicago, and other famous skyscrapers. A separate crew built it under chief Henry Gonzales, while another crew under Dana Yuricich built another version of the clock section of the building at a much larger 1/6 scale.

When the buildings were finished, Joel and Ethan walked among them on the soundstage at Carolco Studios in Wilmington, North Carolina, where they would be shooting. Their old friend William Preston Robertson was visiting and, watching them, he thought they looked like "two waifs lost in FAO Schwartz." No doubt they were excited about the filming to come. But perhaps they were also worried, looking at these amazing million-dollar props. Did they really have a story to justify all this? They could only hope so.

It wasn't only exteriors that had to be built, but the interiors as well. The brothers wanted the offices in the Hudsucker building to be gigantic, as if — so Gassner said — "you were entering Mussolini's [office]." For the basement mailroom (reminiscent of the film Deakins had worked on, *1984*), Gassner arranged 95 mail sorters that had been salvaged in Los Angeles, filling the pigeonholes with 35,000 fake letters.

Now all they had to do was bring in the actors.

Horizontal Buildings

The shoot began in Wilmington in December 1993. Joel, with pony tail and often unshaven on the set, was now 39, Ethan 36, and they were about to make their fifth film — a remarkable record, even if they hadn't drawn a big audience since their second. Due to the complexity of the shooting, a second unit director was needed. Joel didn't like to give up control, but if he had to at least it was to his old friend and the screenplay's cowriter, Sam Raimi. Raimi shot such scenes as the hula hoop rolling down the street and Waring Hudsucker crashing through a window.

But the principal shooting was still done by the brothers. Paul Newman, despite his star status, found that the brothers were no more welcoming of his suggestions than they were of anyone else's. In one scene Newman had to read aloud a memo whose contents as written didn't relate to the story. He suggested making the memo "more germane to the propulsion of the plot." Joel and Ethan said no, giving their reason as "Because we don't want to." Old warhorse that he was, Newman didn't let it bother him. The simple truth was that Joel wasn't looking for deeply felt performances and didn't even try to motivate the actors. Of Newman's role he said, "It's difficult to convey to an actor that he is just supposed to be the bad guy in a melodrama, and not, as is natural, seek to go beyond it." For the most part, Joel was too caught up in making the effects work and getting the style he wanted to worry about the acting. Tim Robbins spent more time getting hula hoop instruction — he had a hard time keeping it up around his waist — than he did talking to the brothers about his character.

Certainly there were many difficult shots to get. Some involved bits of physical comedy, such as Tim Robbins putting his foot into a flaming trash can and hopping around with it. On the first take the fire fizzled out; on the fourth, Robbins fell and banged up his knee. Joel kept the camera constantly moving. The falling sequences — first Charles Durning and then Tim Robbins — had to be filmed against a blue screen, the actors hanging from wires for several hours each. The backgrounds — of buildings flashing by — had to be filmed separately. It turned out to be easier to lay the model buildings sideways and move the camera parallel to the ground to simulate falling. The "approaching" groundscape of street, cars, functioning miniature streetlights, and fire hydrants all had to be made to look real. Norville's fall was complicated by snow falling. Another effect was Waring Hudsucker appearing as an angel to Norville, who has been suspended in his fall by the stopping of time. The Coens wanted the angel to seem partly real and partly mechanical; they had in mind the wings in Terry Gilliam's *Brazil*, a film which also influenced the comically hellish look and pace of the mailroom scenes. The mechanical contraption that designer Peter Chesney came up with had a "deliberate clumsiness" to it. Turkey feathers were hand-sewn onto the frame.

A separate book could easily be devoted to the special effects of *The Hudsucker Proxy*. Just the lighting of the buildings and the face of the Hudsucker clock took great ingenuity. The credits for the film would list many, many more names than for any Coen brothers film before or after. The look of every scene was considered with the most obsessive care, from the snow falling over the roofs of those gorgeous skyscrapers to the bus station where Norville arrives, from the rotating signs of the employment agency to the enormous Hudsucker boardroom. All of it had a lush, almost surreal sheen. The camera movements were so clever and fluid that the viewer could be caught up and entranced by its beautiful gliding vision of this burnished world. At least for a while.

The Big Miscalculation

According to industry reports, the budget for *The Hudsucker Proxy* ballooned from $25 to $40 million. The Coens denied it, although the film certainly looks costly, but whatever the case the film had to do very well at the box office to earn back its investment. Postproduction was headquartered in a hotel called the Shangri-La on Santa Monica Bay in Southern California, a more ordinary place than the name suggests, aside from the view. It was there that they screened an edit that included suggestions by Warner Brothers executives, as they were obligated by contract to do but not necessarily to keep.

While Hollywood routinely test-screens every new picture, showing it to audiences and surveying them afterwards to make editing changes and sometimes even doing reshoots, the Coens had only done it once before: on *Raising Arizona*. Warner Brothers insisted on it this time and the brothers did not object. After all, the film was meant to be a comedy and its success could best be judged by audience response. And besides, they too were nervous and eager for its success not to do whatever they could to help the picture. But the tests came in all over the map, with some audience members liking it and some giving it a big thumbs-down. Using the information as best they could, Joel and

Jennifer Jason Leigh and Tim Robbins at the Cannes Film Festival
STEPHANE BENITO/GLOBE PHOTOS

Ethan added some footage that had been cut from the edit and shot some additional material. The ending especially was added to; it had seemed too rushed.

The new material caused rumors to circulate that "reshoots" were being done to try and save a movie that looked like it was going to be a flop. *Variety* ran with the story — the worst kind of prerelease press. But in truth the industry was already skeptical. The Coens had never had a big commercial hit, and their last two films had done poorly at the box office. *Barton Fink* had divided the critics. Joel and Ethan were considered stylish art-house filmmakers with a small, loyal following. Now they were trying for wide popularity? It just didn't fit the image.

In January 1994, *The Hudsucker Proxy* premiered at the Sundance Film Festival in Park City, an ideal place for launching a new film because of the international media coverage the festival receives. At the press conference Joel Silver appeared nervous; he kept joking that the brothers should use the words "comedy" and "accessible" in their answers as often as possible. Advance attention was good, with major articles appearing all over and

Entertainment Weekly even touting Tim Robbins for an Academy Award nomination. The brothers held their breath and waited.

The filmed opened on March 11 in five select theaters before a wide release (331 screens — a lot for a Coen brothers film) two weeks later. The reviews were disappointing. The critics were not vicious; their judgments carried with them no sense of glee. Most were even appreciative of the spectacular visual effects, the stunning camera work, the references to movie history. But it wasn't enough. The bellwether *Variety* wrote: "*The Hudsucker Proxy* is no doubt one of the most inspired and technically stunning pastiches of old Hollywood pictures ever to come out of the New Hollywood. But a pastiche it remains, as nearly everything in the Coen brothers' latest and biggest film seems like a wizardly but artificial synthesis of aspects of vintage fare, leaving a hole in the middle where some emotion and humanity should be." *Entertainment Weekly*, which had blown up hopes for the film before release, now commented: "How can a filmmaking team be this smart and clever, this restlessly, vivaciously imaginative — and this soulless? . . . These filmmakers are so driven to showcase their precocious formal ingenuity that they end up reducing human experience to a glib, misanthropic cartoon." Likewise Richard Schickel of *Time* called it "heavy, lifeless and dry" and John Powers of *New York* asserted that the Coens had "lost the human dimension of Norville's story in their control-freak obsession with the Hudsucker building's elegant spareness. . . ."

All of these reviews found that the film's stylishness simply wasn't enough, and that the richer emotional content that at least some had seen in *Miller's Crossing* had vanished again. Most thought that the brothers had seriously misread their sources. As Geoff Pevere wrote in the *Globe and Mail*, ". . . this time they've taken on a tradition whose charm has practically nothing to do with its formal properties and everything to do with its percolating spirit." Jonathan Rosenbaum, the Chicago reviewer who was already one of the most articulate social critics of the Coens, once again took exception to the brothers' "contempt for period verisimilitude." He even took offense at the idea that the film derived from Capra and Sturges, writing that the new film "demeans the singularity of both directors." Only a few rare reviews, such as one in *Rolling Stone*, were positive.

Were the reviews right? Had Joel and Ethan been too distracted by, too enamored of their own visual cleverness to see that they'd lost sight of the bigger picture? Were they condescending to the large audience they imagined out there by assuming people would care about Norville and Amy, would hate the evil Mussburger, merely because they were recognizable types? If so, then the brothers truly had missed the point about those 1930s directors Capra, Hawks, and Sturges, each of whom had taken a far more casual approach to the visual qualities of their films. Those directors, whether optimistic like Capra or pessimistic like Sturges, did care about the stories they had to tell. Orson Welles might have had grandiose images dancing in his head when he made *Citizen Kane*, but the images were in the service of some real ideas about politics, society, and personality. Terry Gilliam's *Brazil* was one of the most visually inventive and playful films of our time, but Gilliam too had passionate reasons to create his comically dark world. For *The Hudsucker Proxy* the brothers had no big ideas, no larger social purpose. They didn't even have anything to say about their characters, who, as one critic put it, weren't characters at all but merely "figures." Whether or not a viewer liked the earlier Coen brothers films, they were never dull or unprovocative. At first *The Hudsucker Proxy* was quite thrilling to watch because of the beauty of the images and the clever patter of the dialogue. But by halfway through most viewers found their interest simply sagging; it was impossible to care what happened to Norville, whether he ended up with Amy or not, or even if he really jumped from the window. The story lost all of its tension and for most people the visuals weren't enough.

The film made a paltry $3 to $6 million at American theaters. Warner Brothers lost a huge amount of money while PolyGram, with foreign rights, perhaps broke even in time. Although it was their first real Hollywood film, the brothers couldn't blame the big studio for the flop. And to their credit, Joel and Ethan never tried, nor did they point a finger at Joel Silver. Joel said, "We don't have anyone to blame for the weaknesses but ourselves."

A setback though it was, the failure of *The Hudsucker Proxy* was not about to put the brothers' career on hold. They had already been planning their next, much smaller film — a good thing since they would likely not have been able to raise another large budget. Hollywood opinion was that Joel and Ethan were still a class team whose reputation would lift any studio. At least as long as the price wasn't too high.

As for the brothers' egos, they seemed intact as Joel and Ethan publicly accepted and at the same time shrugged off the failure. According to some, however, they were hiding how upset they really were, and their fears that opportunities might be narrowing for them. And while they had had box-office duds before, this was their first film that was universally seen as an artistic flop. Artistic failure, however, is not something to be ashamed of. All artists who take risks crash sometimes. In the end what seems most constructive about the failure of *The Hudsucker Proxy* is how Joel and Ethan learned that they could not simply crib character types from early movies and expect the audience to attach the appropriate emotions so that the brothers could concentrate on what really interested them. Seeing that the film was not going to succeed, Joel said, "It's almost axiomatic that a movie's principal characters have to be sympathetic, and that the movie has to supply moral uplift. People like it. But it's not interesting to us." Fair enough. But perhaps the mistake was in pretending that they did.

CHAPTER EIGHT

BLOOD ON THE SNOW

FARGO

"I guess that was your accomplice in the woodchipper."
— Marge in *Fargo*

It would be easy to assume that after the debacle of *The Hudsucker Proxy*, Joel and Ethan would choose to retreat to a film with their smallest budget in years in order to lick their wounds. And also that the story they chose, a thriller closer to *Blood Simple* than any of their other films, was an attempt to return to their earliest success. But that wasn't exactly the case. For one thing, it was the expensive film that was the anomaly; making a cheaper film was not a retreat but a return to the norm. For another, the next screenplay that they wrote — before the release of *The Hudsucker Proxy* — did not turn out to be the next film they actually made.

The screenplay the brothers wrote was called *The Big Lebowski*. After finishing it they decided that Jeff Bridges was the perfect actor for the lead role. The only problem was that Bridges was tied up with other film commitments; if the brothers wanted him they would just have to wait. So Joel and

Ethan put the screenplay away and wrote another.

The new film that would become *Fargo* was — or so the brothers said, both in interviews and at the start of the film — based on reality. "This is a true story," rolled the words on the screen. "The events depicted in this film took place in Minnesota in 1987. At the request of the survivors, the names have been changed. Out of respect for the dead, the rest has been told exactly as it occurred." Some of the critics took them at their word, while others were doubtful, especially since the film also carried a disclaimer at the end about the characters being fictional. Was the story of a Minnesota car salesman so in debt that he hires two thugs to kidnap his wife based on an actual occurrence? On at least one occasion the brothers said that the events really did happen, but not in Minnesota. To his old friend William Preston Robertson, Ethan said that it was "mostly made-up" and that "There are more elements that are actually true in *The Big Lebowski* than there were in *Fargo*." After the film was released a Minnesota newspaper sent out a reporter to find out if there really had been such a kidnapping and murder in the state. The reporter couldn't find any trace of one.

If this evidence wasn't enough, one can also turn to Ethan's introduction to the published screenplay. In it he recounted a "true" story told by the brothers' grandmother, and then questioned whether or not it could possibly have happened the way she told it. He concluded this way: "The story that follows is about Minnesota. It evokes the abstract landscape of our childhood — a bleak, windswept tundra, resembling Siberia except for its Ford dealerships and Hardee's restaurants. It aims to be both homey and exotic; and pretends to be true."

So where did the story come from? While mostly fictional, it does seem to have germinated from an actual event. Back in 1987 — the year in which the film is set — the brothers mentioned in an interview reading a newspaper account of a man in Connecticut who put his wife in a woodchipper. "That was a good one," the brothers agreed, laughing weirdly. There was no mention of a car salesman in debt or a kidnapping or of hired thugs or of any other deaths. The news item seems to have been merely a catalyst for their own convoluted and grisly tale. Calling it a "true story" helped to give it the air of reality that they wanted in this, their most naturalistic film. The brothers, who occasionally liked to use fictional names in their credits, probably also thought it would be fun to deceive the audience.

Instead of Connecticut, the brothers decided to set the film, despite its title, in Minnesota. While they were hardly autobiographical filmmakers, they thought it was time to depict an area and a sensibility that they felt they knew well. As Ethan would say, "The landscapes, the characters, and the overall Midwestern sensibilities" were very familiar to them. One of their main impulses was to move away from the "self-consciously artificial style" of their last two pictures, as Joel put it, and towards one that was more realistic. The character of Jerry Lundegaard, the car salesman, came in part from a real sales-man Ethan had encountered while buying a car some time before. He claimed that the infuriating conversation with a couple about TruCoat — worthy of a David Mamet play — was taken almost verbatim from his encounter. But that again was just the beginning. What interested the brothers was, in Ethan's words, "the psychology of a person who constructs those pyramid financial schemes but can't project themselves a minute into the future or imagine the consequences." The comment points to a marked difference in the brothers' approach to this screenplay; for once they were more interested in depicting characters as "real" people rather than stylized types from literature and other films. As Joel said, they wanted to "speculate about the individual motivations, intentions, actions, and reactions," of a group of more realistic figures. They saw their two main characters, Jerry and Marge, as ordinary people caught up in an extraordinary situation.

They certainly hadn't created a character like Marge before. "We wanted her as far away as possible from the cliché cop," Joel said. "Marge and Jerry are both very banal, like the interiors and the landscape. But she is banal in a good way, a good person where he is evil. We wanted to give them everyday concerns. Being pregnant: you can't get more ordinary." Joel's wife, Frances McDormand, who would play Marge, felt that until *Fargo* the brothers' characterizations of women always had "something missing from them," and it was certainly true that their forte was writing two-handed male scenes. Until Marge, they had almost shied away from writing women characters; the least developed role in *Blood Simple*, for example, was the woman at the center of the story. Now they wanted to create a strong female character who relished her ordinary life with a dull but loving husband even as she spent her days pursuing people with mur-derous intentions. Making Marge pregnant was a simple but extraordinarily rich notion; it would color everything the character did and said. In a way, it is a variation and a fulfillment of Edwina in *Raising Arizona*, the woman who desperately wanted but couldn't have children. And it would win the kind of sympathy from the audience that the brothers usually seemed cynical about.

These two "banal" characters would play a cat-and-mouse game as they became involved in an extraordinary series of events that somehow grow larger than either of them. The kidnapping had evolved from the one in *Raising Arizona*, although it was only later that the brothers noticed that kidnapping was becoming something of a theme. Joel traced it back to a Kurosawa film he loved, *High and Low*, which he called "probably the best kidnapping movie ever made." Possibly it also sprung from a 1978 Elmore Leonard novel called *The Switch*, which, as critic Robert Fulford has noted, employs a scam very similar to Jerry's. As the brothers were fans of Leonard's kind of detective fiction, and had a history of borrowing novel plots, the influence seems possible. In fact, later they would even work on direct adaptations of Leonard novels.

The brothers began writing as soon as the shoot for *The Hudsucker Proxy* was done. The script first sets the bleak scene — a fade from white to a car travelling down an empty highway that crosses a flat, snowbound landscape — then launches immediately into the plot, beginning with a meeting between Jerry and the thugs where the kidnapping of Jerry's wife is arranged. From the beginning the dialogue is scintillating as Jerry, genial on the surface but with a desperate panic bubbling under the surface, has to argue the value of his scheme. The ransom money will be paid by Jerry's rich father-in-law, and Jerry and the thugs will all get a share. Only later will we understand that Jerry owes $320,000 to the bank, having taken out a loan with some nonexistent cars as collateral. What he needed the original cash for, we are never informed.

Cut to the Lundegaard home and Jerry's mousy wife and oppressively dominant father-in-law, Wade, who was based on businessmen the brothers met while raising money in Minnesota for their first film. In one of his other schemes, Jerry is trying to get Wade to loan him money for a parking lot. Next we see Jerry at work, forcing a couple into accepting an extra charge on their new car for TruCoat sealant; but his mind is occupied with his problems. In the meantime, Carl and Gaear get closer to their victim, stopping in a pancake house, picking up a couple of hookers at a motel room, arguing in the car Jerry has given them — or rather Carl is neurotically talking while Gaear refuses to speak. The kidnapping scene is both comic and horrific, as Jerry's terrified wife tries to escape her masked pursuers through her house, getting caught up in the shower curtain and falling down the stairs.

While Wade tries to screw Jerry out of his parking lot deal, Carl and Gaear's getaway goes seriously wrong. Stopped by a state trooper, the more murderous Gaear shoots the trooper dead and then hunts down two witnesses in a passing car, executing one in her overturned car and shooting the other in the back.

Only now does a late-night phone call introduce us to the screenplay's heroine, Marge Gunderson, sleeping next to her husband Norm — who insists on getting up to make her breakfast before she goes. Marge is a cop and also pregnant, simple of speech but with clever deductive powers. When she visits the murder scene by the road, she throws up, not from the gruesome sight of the bodies but from morning sickness — a nice detail suggested later by Frances McDormand. It is her ordinary decency that makes her so endearing. When a fellow cop makes a deductive error, she corrects him and then tells a joke to cover up his embarrassment.

Jerry manages to convince Wade to pay the ransom money without calling the cops, while Marge begins her detective work, tracking down the two none-too-bright prostitutes, and searching for other clues. She is shown eating with her husband, a pleasant, rather dull painter of wildfowl for postage stamps whom Marge obviously adores; the brothers decided to write several eating scenes into the script, especially with Marge and Norm, to enhance the ordinariness of Marge's life. "It is that peculiarly Middle American thing about mounds of food," Ethan said.

Now with three deaths on their hands, Carl and Gaear, holed up with Jerry's wife in a cabin in the woods, demand more money from Jerry. Just before the ransom hand-off, Wade decides to take over from his son-in-law, only to end up dead on a rooftop — but not before shooting Carl in the jaw. Carl kills the rooftop parking-lot attendant as well. In a narrative aside, Marge has a drink at the local Radisson Hotel with an old high school mate, a Korean-American who makes a pass at her and then weeps about missing his dead wife. Later Marge discovers that Mike has never married but has a history of mental problems. This seemingly unnecessary strand heightens Marge's sense of her good fortune in life and gives her a further glimpse into the bizarre complexities of the human personality. Ethan claimed that the subplot was part of their "experimenting with naturalism."

Following her clues, Marge meets Jerry at the car dealership to ask about a missing car, but Jerry responds in a strange and unhelpful manner. When she returns a second time, Jerry flees the scene.

His jaw bleeding, and in severe pain, Carl buries the extra ransom money by a fence post in a snowy field, and returns to the cabin to discover that Gaear has killed Jerry's wife. Carl and Gaear argue about who will keep the car; then, outside the cabin, Gaear kills Carl with an ax. Having put the various pieces together, Marge comes upon the cabin, where, just outside, Gaear is feeding Carl's body into a woodchipper, pushing his foot into it with a log. She manages to arrest and handcuff Gaear and gets him into the backseat of her cruiser. Her intelligence has led her to solve the crime but not to understand the perpetrators. "And for what?" she asks the silent Gaear. "For a little bit of money." The screenplay does not end here, however, but with Marge and Norm in bed. Norm announces that his painting of a mallard will grace the three-cent stamp. It is a mild disappointment to him since the three-cent isn't used much, but Marge assures him it's a terrific accomplishment. Then they think of the coming baby. "Two more months," says Marge.

Since *Blood Simple*, the brothers had not given Joel's wife, Frances McDormand, a major role, but now they wrote the part of Marge especially for her. Other characters were also written with specific actors in mind. For the psychotic hyperactive talker Carl Showalter it was Steve Buscemi, an actor for whom they had previously found only small roles, who they wanted. His partner, Gaear, was meant for Peter Stormare, in part because the brothers wanted to use one real Scandinavian actor among all these characters of Scandinavian descent.

Which brings us to the question of dialect. Joel and Ethan liked writing in the dialects of different Americans, from the drawling Texan of *Blood Simple* to the intellectual urban Jew in *Barton Fink* to the black southern narrator of *The Hudsucker Proxy*. None of these were intended to be strictly realistic; they were all stylized or caricatured to a greater or lesser degree. In the screenplay for *Fargo* they tackled the dialect that they had often heard around them growing up in Minnesota, a Midwestern set of expressions tinged with a Scandinavian lilt due to the large number of Swedish immigrants. The brothers did not merely rely on memory, but used a book by Howard Mohr of the radio show *A Prairie Home Companion* called *How To Talk Minnesotan*, which helped them sprinkle the characters' lines with "you betcha," "oh geez," "yah sure," "yah think?" and other expressions. Copies of the book were even given to the actors on the set to help them get the rhythm right. As always, the brothers weren't trying to be absolutely realistic; they wanted to use the accent to achieve a heightened sense of locality — unusual in American films where characters are usually "ethnically invisible," as a comment in *Sight and Sound* put it — to increase the sense of ordinariness among the locals, and, of course, to be funny.

The brothers finished the script in three months. Shooting would begin only three months after that, an amazingly short time from script to filming, and a noteworthy contrast to the years it took to make *The Hudsucker Proxy*, whose genuine energy may have seeped away over time to be replaced by a sort of frantic busyness. In contrast, everything about *Fargo* seemed charmed. Everything, that is, except the snow.

Back to Small

After the Invasion of Normandy–sized production of *The Hudsucker Proxy*, the brothers found it a relief to prepare for a little skirmish like *Fargo*. While filming *Hudsucker*, the brothers had talked with Tim Bevan and Eric Fellner of Working Title about future projects, and the partners had loved the script of *Fargo* when they read it. Nor was making a commitment very painful: with a budget of only $6.5 million, it was the Coens' least expensive film since *Raising Arizona* and only a fraction of *Hudsucker*'s budget. So, while Warner Brothers dropped out of the deal for the new film, PolyGram and Working Title stayed in and Gramercy Pictures came on board as the North American distributor.

With a budget that small, the brothers could not expect to hire stars on the order of Paul Newman and Tim Robbins or even Gabriel Byrne or Nicolas Cage. But that was all right with them; Joel and Ethan were happy working with less familiar faces. In the introduction to the published screenplay of *The Hudsucker Proxy*, which was purportedly an interview with producer Joel Silver but was actually penned by the brothers, Silver is made to say that the brothers consider it "a sin to use a movie star" and hadn't wanted Paul Newman because he was too "iconic."

Of course it was easy to cast Marge, since the part had been written for

A great part at last for
Steve Buscemi
BEN MARK HOLZBERG/
SHOOTING STAR

"I can't stand
emotional acting":
William H. Macy
HENRY MCGEE/
GLOBE PHOTOS

Frances McDormand. McDormand had become wary, and sometimes even resentful, at Joel and Ethan's reluctance to consider her for leading roles, so she must have been surprised when they simply handed her a copy of the script and said, "Here you go, here's Marge." Later she joked, "It's the first time in 12 years of sleeping with the director that I got the job, no questions asked." McDormand did no research on female police officers or anything else for the part, but just decided to trust her instincts, although she may have unconsciously drawn from her own sister, a chaplain in a women's maximum-security prison. To her, Marge was the first woman created by the brothers who was a fully rounded character. While she was "representative" of the typically Midwestern acceptance of life at face value and tendency to be content, there was also more to her. "She has an inner life that is not immediately evident but which keeps revealing itself," McDormand said. "There's something scary about Marge that's hard to articulate. She's simple and on-the-surface, but she's not naïve, and she's not innocent, because she's good at her job, which gives her contact with crime and murder. But she has absolutely no understanding of why people do the terrible things they do."

Marge was certainly the overt star of the picture, in large part because she was an unlikely heroine. But the real engine of the film was Jerry Lundegaard, its hapless villain. Really it was the contrast of the two, moving in parallel through the story, that made the screenplay so fascinating to follow. When the actor William H. Macy read the script, he thought, "*Fargo* was the best thing I had read in a long time. I essentially begged these guys to cast me as Jerry."

Born in Miami in 1950 and raised in Atlanta, Macy began acting in high school. His formative influence was his acting teacher at college in Vermont, a budding playwright named David Mamet, who had a very definite and restrained, even minimalist, approach to acting. When Mamet went to Chicago, Macy followed him and the two were close friends during the early hungry years; there's a famous long monologue in Mamet's first great play, *American Buffalo*, that was inspired by Macy sarcastically telling Mamet to "help yourself" to the last piece of Velveeta cheese in Macy's fridge. Macy eventually got steady work in Chicago, where he began to make a decent living doing television commercials, as well as acting in Mamet's plays. Then it was on to New York and 20 years of skillful and dependable acting in theater and films, including *Benny & Joon, Searching for Bobby Fischer, Mr. Holland's Opus*, and several Mamet films, including *Homicide*. He also worked as an occasional director and even writer, co-writing an episode of *Thirtysomething* and an HBO movie called *Above Suspicion*. He was best known to larger audiences, however, for the continuing role of Dr. Morgenstern on the television show *ER*.

Of slight build, Macy is physically remarkable for his expressive face — a wide mouth, large ears, and a road-map of lines around his eyes. What probably appealed to the brothers was the way Macy could appear to be holding in a volcanic buildup of emotions — so appropriate for the frustrations and angers and fears that Jerry is trying to contain beneath a barely controlled facade. "I can't stand emotional acting," Macy has said, "with people weeping and getting all upset when they act. It's just unpleasant to watch. I don't like it in real life and I don't like it in the theater, so I don't do it." About Jerry he commented, "The thing I loved most about Jerry is the fact that he never gives up. He sets the plan, he is sure it will work, and despite all information to the contrary, he never deviates from it. Up to the very last scene in the movie, he's still fighting to make it work. You've just gotta love somebody that has this kind of faith. On the other hand, he's as dumb as a bag of rocks, and I liked that too."

Probably the next most important role was that of Carl Showalter, which went to Steve Buscemi. Finally the brothers had given the actor, who had made a specialty of fast-talking lowlifes, a part to throw himself into. Buscemi had been busy lately, making *Desperado*, *Things to do in Denver When You're Dead*, *Living in Oblivion*, and *Somebody to Love* — but he hadn't yet had a part this rich. Peter Stormare, his chilling partner in crime as Gaear Grimsrud, was well known in his native Sweden, where he had often performed with and directed plays by the National Theater. For Ingmar Bergman he had acted in the film *Fanny and Alexander*, while in England he had made *Damage* and in America *Awakenings*. Very tall and strong-looking, with sleek blond hair and a long face, he could send chills through viewers with one cold-blooded yet disturbingly blank expression.

Jerry's overpowering father-in-law Wade went to Harve Presnell, an actor well known for roles on Broadway and in the films *Paint Your Wagon* and *The Unsinkable Molly Brown*, but who had not been seen on the screen for 25 years. When it came to films, the brothers had a long memory. Many of the other actors, such as John Carroll Lynch, who was cast as Marge's sweet and mild husband Norm, came from the Tyrone Guthrie Theater in Minneapolis, a conveniently nearby source for talent.

With Roger Deakins signed on again as cinematographer, the brothers worked on the storyboards with him and the artist J. Todd Anderson. Feeling more self-assured than when they began filmmaking, they didn't storyboard every scene, leaving the uncomplicated ones to be worked out on the set. They called on a new production designer, Rick Heinrichs, who had previously worked on *Batman Returns*, *Edward Scissorhands*, and other demanding films. Less obviously a "designed" film than the last couple of Coen brothers pictures, *Fargo* was nevertheless to be a stylized version of Minnesota with its bland interiors, neon signs, endless fences, and its feeling of a limitless landscape of undifferentiated snow and sky. Heinrichs was also responsible for building the ominous and possibly symbolic statue of Paul Bunyan.

The costume designer was also new, unfortunately for tragic reasons. Richard Hornung, the Coens' regular designer, had expected to do the film but became too ill with AIDS. He recommended his assistant, Mary Zophres, who had worked on the last two films but until now hadn't had much personal contact with the brothers. Joel described the look they wanted this way: "Everyone is bulked-up, moving in a particular way, bouncing off people. That sponginess is part of the regional flavor. Marge's pregnancy [by means of a false "pad"] means she's doubly bulked-up. She's of the region, but is capable, which the other characters aren't. She wears a funny hat and walks funny, but she isn't a clown." William H. Macy added his own touch to his regulation salesman's jacket — a pin testifying to five years service as a car salesman that he insisted on wearing in every scene.

During preproduction, the brothers fine-tuned the script. A few cuts were made, notably a scream sequence. After that Joel and Ethan were ready to shoot.

Looking For Snow

For the first time in their career, the brothers filmed in and around their hometown of Minneapolis. They used sites known since childhood, such as the Embers Restaurant in St. Louis Park, where Ethan had worked as a dishwasher when he was a teenager. Shooting began on January 23, 1995, the heart of winter, to ensure them of the snow they needed. To keep warm Joel wore a hat with earflaps much like Marge's, a bulky jacket, and gloves; Roger Deakins kept his

Roger Deakins on the set of *Fargo* with the Coen brothers

Joel directs his wife Frances McDormand in a scene from *Fargo*

own hat pulled down, and the rest of the crew were well wrapped. Having worked on *Barton Fink* and then *The Hudsucker Proxy*, Deakins found it something of a relief to have a smaller crew and more flexibility. He used as much natural light as possible and real locations rather than sets to add to the sense of realism. The brothers let him use longer lenses and make the camera work less showy and noticeable; this time they wanted the camera to be a calm and neutral observer of the action. Wearing his director's hat, Joel said, "The key thing about the exteriors was that we couldn't see the line between the sky and the snow. Up angles would be very similar to down angles; we wanted to have this void, blank, featureless look in which we put in certain graphic details." The challenge for Deakins was to get that look without visually boring the audience.

Frances McDormand had made herself look very dowdy for the role, wanting to come down on the side of "truthfulness." Seeing her, Joel told her that she didn't have to look quite *that* dowdy, but McDormand insisted. During the first week of the shoot she and Joel had to work out a professional relationship again, putting aside their personal life together. She even took a separate hotel room. Besides, she groaned, during a shoot Joel's room was always a mess, with dirty laundry scattered about — an offense to her natural tidiness. While they shot, Joel encouraged her to make Marge more open and warm. McDormand, on the other hand, worried about making her a caricature.

The biggest problem of the shoot turned out to be not the actors but the weather. The winter of 1995 would be known as one of the mildest in Minnesota history. The crew had to manufacture snow and finally, on March 9, pull up stakes from the Twin Cities and head further north, to the Grand Forks area of North Dakota. Good fortune prevailed; just enough snow fell there to finish the exterior scenes and head back to Minneapolis on March 20 for a final day of shooting. Warm weather or not, the landscape that the brothers and Roger Deakins captured on film looked just as blankly white and bleak as they could have hoped for.

A Surprise Hit

By now the Coens' composer, Carter Burwell, had experience drawing on folk sources for his soundtracks. He had used Irish tunes for *Miller's Crossing* and now for *Fargo* he drew on an old Scandinavian hymn, "The Last Sheep," which he arranged more grandly for orchestra. He employed other elements of Scandinavian music as well, such as the "hardanger" fiddle. And the film drew on some period pop music, from "Do You Know the Way to San Jose" to "Up, Up and Away."

Under their old pseudonym of Roderick Jaynes, the brothers cut the film themselves with the help of Ethan's wife, Tricia. After *Hudsucker*, it must have been a pleasure to be able to retain so much control themselves. One scene left on the cutting-room floor was a scene with a real local Minneapolis TV talk-show host named Bill Carlson, a friend of the brothers. Carlson played a local news anchor, but the brothers decided that nobody outside the Minneapolis area would get the joke.

Fargo was ready for release in the spring of 1996. By this time Ethan and Tricia had moved to an area of Manhattan near the East River called Kips Bay, while Joel and Frances were still on the Upper West Side, near the brothers' office on Riverside Drive. A preacher's daughter at heart, Frances had decorated their place with heavy, even old-fashioned, furniture. The real change was that now both couples had become families; in their eerie twinlike way, the brothers had become fathers at almost exactly the same time. Two months after the *Fargo* shoot had wrapped Joel and Frances had gone to Paraguay to adopt a baby boy named Pedro. It was the culmination of McDormand's lifelong desire to be a mother. And Ethan's wife, Tricia, had given birth to their son Buster in late December of the same year. The boys from St. Louis Park had grown up.

Given that Joel and Ethan expected the usual mixed response and small audience for their new film, they must have been pleasantly surprised by the pre-release review in *Variety*. The lead review, it praised the brothers for managing "the precarious balancing act of respecting genre conventions [the crime-gone-wrong] and simultaneously pushing them to an almost surrealist extreme." The critic pronounced the film "very funny," with a "first-rate cast." Even the editor, Roderick Jaynes, was lauded. "*Fargo* is a strikingly mature, unique entertainment that plays on many levels . . . all satisfying."

All satisfying? A film by the Coen brothers, who seemed to tantalize and infuriate critics in equal proportion? Who until now had teased but never satisfied? But of course this was only the verdict of one critic — and one that the industry rather than the general public read. The brothers waited.

In retrospect it almost seems as if many critics — admirers of the Coens but up to now unable to fully embrace any single film — were just waiting for *Fargo*. Janet Maslin wrote in the all-important *New York Times* that the film recalled their first, *Blood Simple*, only it was "much more stylish and entertaining." She called Marge "a folk hero" and noted both the film's humor and its "sharp ferocity." It was the Coen brothers' best film yet, she pronounced.

So also said *Entertainment Weekly*'s Lisa Schwarzbaum. Calling it a "dizzily rich, witty, and satisfying new movie," she pointedly raised the issue of whether the Coens' films have lacked emotional content. "If Marge represents everything in a person that's decent, compassionate, competent, and lovable to these filmmaking brothers, then you know what? The guys have their hearts in the right place, not just their clever heads." The praise went on and on. *Interview* declared it a "masterful black comedy"; the *Toronto Star* called it "the first great movie of the year, you betcha." (Most critics couldn't help dropping some Minnesota-speak into their reviews.) The very few negative reviews were mere exceptions that proved the rule. The *Village Voice*, having established the Coens as Enemy Number 1, published an inane review that called watching the film a "thankless task." *Time*'s Richard Corliss asserted that the brothers showed "giddy contempt toward people who talk and think Minnesotan." To him, they were making low fun of their characters.

Mr. Corliss must have seemed rather out of step to his readers. Before long, word of mouth had it that *Fargo* was the film to see. Audience members came out sprinkling their talk with "Oh geeze" and "You betcha." The film was attracting the brothers' largest audience since *Raising Arizona*, a terrific jump from their last pictures. And then the nominations and awards started coming — a Best Screenplay award to Joel and Ethan from the Los Angeles Film Critics Association, and another from the Writers Guild of America, among others. For the public, though, none could compare with the Academy Awards. And when the nominations were announced, *Fargo* received a total of seven, all of them in major categories: Best Picture, Best Director (Joel), Best Original Screenplay (Ethan and Joel), Best Actress (Frances McDormand), Best Supporting Actor (William H. Macy), Best Cinematography (Roger Deakins), and Best Editor ("Roderick Jaynes").

This was a tremendous feat for a small-budget film with no stars. No stars, that is, before opening, for it brought sudden fame to both McDormand and Macy. Having worked so long and hard, Macy found it pleasant indeed to be suddenly in demand. Scripts flooded his agent; he would soon sign on for first-rate roles in such films as *Air Force One, Wag the Dog, Pleasantville, A Civil Action,* and *Mystery Men.* "I'm at the grown-ups' table for sure now," he beamed. But at the moment it seemed as if everyone was talking about *Fargo,* not just movie critics and film majors and people who deliberately avoided Hollywood movies for more offbeat material. Moviegoers wanted to see it before Oscar night.

Of course a long-time Coen brothers admirer might have been slightly annoyed by all this belated attention. The brothers had finally made a more realistic picture with a likable heroine and suddenly everyone was a fan. What about the sharp-as-a-knife noiresque plotting of *Blood Simple?* What about the rural philosophizing and surreal comedy of *Raising Arizona?* Or the grandly subversive gangster melodrama, *Miller's Crossing?* The darkly comic nightmare of *Barton Fink,* the hyper-clever, gorgeous shamming of *The Hudsucker Proxy?* These films were fascinating precisely *because* they confounded audience expectations. They made viewers uneasy; they undermined the audience's natural desire to *believe* what was up on the screen. They refused to take themselves seriously, and yet they could provoke heated — and serious — discussions about the nature of evil, of violence, of human desire, and of the imagination.

All true enough, but the less conventionally "satisfying" achievements of the earlier films did not take away from the spectacularly satisfying *Fargo.* Besides, although *Fargo* was more outwardly realistic, a person didn't have to do much more than scratch the surface to reveal the trademark Coen brothers' style. A pregnant cop on the track of murderers? A monstrously overbearing father-in-law taking things into his own hands and being killed for his trouble? A petty crook who can't stop talking and ends up, in gruesomely fitting manner, being shot in the jaw? A murderer stuffing the limbs of his accomplice into a wood-chipper, seemingly to hide the body but instead turning the snow all around red with blood and guts? And the imagery: a car bursting through the whiteness of snow on an empty highway; a bleeding man digging by a line of fence posts stretching off into bleak infinity; a woman bursting through a shower curtain and screaming. Much of this was ugly but also, like all Coen brothers' films, unnervingly funny too. And as for the film's supposed warmth, it is true that the film ends with Marge cozily in bed with her husband Norm. "Heck, we're doin' pretty good, Norm," Marge says to her hubby, and we are both amused and comforted. It is the ending that Hi dreams of at the end of *Raising Arizona,* now

Peter Stormare,
Frances McDormand,
and Steve Buscemi
looking appropriately
chic for the Cannes
Film Festival
RON DAVIS/
SHOOTING STAR

come to life for another couple. It is tempting to speculate that it has emerged from the brothers' own desires — now fulfilled — to have children of their own. If this makes the film easier to like, then so be it. It isn't so bad to know that the world does not solely consist of murderous jealousy, fanatical need, monstrous egotism, and flat-out cynicism.

The only people who didn't seem overly pleased with the success of *Fargo* were some of the good people of Minnesota. All those "Yer darn tootin"s and "You betcha"s turned out to be offensive to touchy Minnesotans who felt, as the reviewer in *Time* did, that they were being made fun of. A Twin Cities talk-radio station held a two-hour show on whether the film was insulting or not; callers jammed the lines with complaints. The *Minneapolis Star Tribune* printed a warning that "Many Minnesotans may be offended by parts of *Fargo*." Reluctantly, the brothers publicly commented. The *Brainerd Daily Dispatch*, hometown paper for one of the locations in the film, quoted Joel as saying, "It's a little bit strange to us, because certainly there was no intention to lampoon the characters in the movie." He went on to say that he and Ethan considered themselves

Minnesotans and a product of the state's culture. As well, they felt affection towards the characters. Perhaps because the audience laughs at their mistakes, they are misinterpreting this humor as condescension.

Joel and Ethan had another, more amusing, little problem on their hands. What would they do if their alter ego, Roderick Jaynes, the aging and blustery English editor they had fabricated, actually won an Oscar? Deciding to play it safe, the brothers approached the Academy and asked whether they could hire an actor to play Jaynes. The answer was a regretful no. Proxies had been disallowed ever since the infamous night when Marlon Brando had sent up Sacheen Littlefeather in his absence. Then the cat was let out of the bag when a reporter for *Variety* went looking for Jaynes and discovered that there was no such member of the American Cinema Editors organization.

In March came the night of the Academy Awards. Roderick Jaynes didn't win, but *Fargo* fans were thrilled when Frances McDormand's name was called for Best Actress. As she hadn't expected to win — Brenda Blethyn for *Secrets and Lies* or Kristin Scott Thomas for *The English Patient* seemed like better bets — McDormand was caught by surprise. In fact, she was a popular choice; people had embraced the character of Marge and McDormand was seen as a Hollywood outsider in the best sense of the term.

Without question the actress was thrilled with the win, and glad to know that someone who had never felt like part of the Hollywood community could still be recognized. But she was a private and modest person, and her response afterwards, faced with even more media attention, was to retreat into her life as a mother and her work in New York for the 52nd Street Project, bringing kids and theater professionals together in the Hispanic neighborhood of Hell's Kitchen. She was also studying Spanish so that she could give Pedro a sense of his heritage. For a while she even turned down acting parts and refused most interviews and appearances.

Fargo won a second Academy Award that night when the brothers themselves were honored for their screenplay. As might be expected, they gave pretty lame, mumbling speeches. In fact, like McDormand, Joel and Ethan just weren't comfortable with the attention. Added to that was a natural cynicism about such things as fame and the media. The brothers were actually in production for their next film, *The Big Lebowski*, and Jeff Bridges, the lead in the new picture, couldn't help noticing how much the brothers squirmed under the attention. "I did yank their chains about it a little bit, yeah," he said with a big smile. When asked about it, the brothers were sheepish about admitting that the attention was annoying and even difficult; it made them seem like bad winners. "Well, who knows?" Ethan said of the supposed positive effect of the awards. "You know specifically how it figured as a nuisance. You don't know specifically what it gained you, since you don't know how easy it would have been to raise money for your next film absent that . . . the nuisance part we're sure of." And Joel added, "It's not like it was such a horrible thing. It's just that we were in the middle of production of *The Big Lebowski* and it's a bit distracting when everyone around you is breathing heavily about this other thing."

Actually, it wasn't as impossible as Ethan suggested to know the effects of the awards; all one had to do was look at the box-office numbers after the nominations and then, again, after Oscar night. No doubt there was a noticeable rise both times. With all the attention and awards, however, it was easy for people to assume that the Coen brothers had a financial smash with *Fargo* — perhaps even one of the top-grossing films of the year. It wasn't true. The film did very well for Joel and Ethan, but with a U.S. box office of $25 million, it didn't come close to the year's biggest moneymakers, which broke the $100-million mark. Even so, *Fargo* made about five times more than *The Hudsucker Proxy* did, and on a much smaller budget. There was no doubt that *Fargo* was a very profitable film, and that as producers, directors, and writers, the brothers made some very substantial money on it.

The brothers had finally found a larger audience. It would be interesting to see whether they could keep it.

A peculiar addendum to the story of *Fargo* was the television show of the same name. Made by PolyGram Television, the TV arm of the company that coproduced the film, it was originally sold to NBC but then, when the station changed its mind, moved to CBS. PolyGram thought that the basic components of the movie — a female cop solving crimes in a Midwest populated with eccentrics — would reproduce nicely on the small screen week after week. Theoretically, it already had something of a presold audience in all the movie's fans. In fact, there was a mini-boom of film-based shows in production, including *The Player* and *Dirty Rotten Scoundrels*. Joel and Ethan agreed to the series, and to act as consultants, but otherwise it was in the hands of executive producer

Bruce Paltrow, a creator of *St. Elsewhere*. The cast was not well known (a then unknown actress named Edie Falco was cast as Marge), but behind the camera were some veterans of quality television, including cinematographer John S. Bartley of *The X-Files* for the pilot. Director of the pilot was the actress Kathy Bates (winner of an Oscar for her performance in *Misery*) who had recently turned to directing. Filming took place in April 1997 in Edmonton, Alberta, where costs were lower and the snow supposedly more reliable. But like the film, the crew of the pilot was plagued by an unexpected warm spell.

In the end, the series did not get picked up and only the pilot was made and aired. None of the other film-based series fared any better. Joel and Ethan, who had never expressed any interest in working for television, could not have been much fazed. Besides, they were too busy making movies.

CHAPTER NINE

CALIFORNIA STORY

THE BIG LEBOWSKI

"Lebowski: Is it . . . is it, being prepared to do the right thing?
Whatever the price? Isn't that what makes a man?
Dude: That, and a pair of testicles." — *The Big Lebowski*

With *Fargo* in the can, the brothers could now return to the screenplay they had written before it, *The Big Lebowski*. It was more stylized than *Fargo*, with characters who tended to speechify in traditional Coen brothers fashion, and it combined the philosophical and the goofy as only the brothers could. As they imagined the film, it would be more of a visual and conceptual escapade in the manner of previous films. But it was lighter in spirit, a comedy without the darker overtones, perhaps in spirit like a more sophisticated *Raising Arizona*. What it shared most with *Fargo* was a concern for more rounded and appealing characters and a downplaying of the ironic and cynical tone they were known for and which could be both interesting and distancing.

Joel and Ethan had already drawn on James M. Cain and Dashiell Hammett as inspirations for films (*Blood Simple* and *Miller's Crossing* respectively). Now it was time to call up the spirit of the third writer in their triumvirate — Raymond Chandler. More precisely, it was Chandler's *The Big Sleep* they wanted to parallel, if in a joking way, in their own *Big* movie. Although they drew some of the plot and the characters of the Big Lebowski himself, his wife, and his daughter from the book, what the brothers really liked was the relative insignificance of the shambling, hopelessly complex plot — even Chandler himself didn't know who committed one of the murders in the novel. Instead, it was the characters and the atmosphere of Los Angeles that made Chandler's book so entrancing. "We wanted to do a Chandler kind of story in terms of how it moves, episodically in terms of the characters, unraveling a mystery," Joel said. "And also about it being about Los Angeles in terms of the way Chandler's stories are." They were also influenced by Robert Altman's film adaptation of another Chandler novel, *The Long Goodbye*, with Elliott Gould as a shabby, less-than-sharp private eye with a tendency to make absurd speeches.

The brothers had lived in L.A. twice — once in the early days with Sam Raimi, and again during the filming of *Barton Fink* — and while they considered themselves "tourists there" they had picked up enough of a sense of the place to imagine it as a setting for some very particular characters. In fact, they had met the models for those characters while living in L.A., types that they just couldn't imagine existing anywhere else but in that sunny land of complete informalness and surreal juxtapositions. One of them, the inspiration for the screenplay's hero, Jeff "The Dude" Lebowski, was an independent film producer's rep named Jeff Dowd, also nicknamed "the Dude." Like their fictional creation, the real Jeff had once been a member of an activist group called the Seattle Seven. He liked to call himself "the Pope of dope"; the brothers' Dude would also enjoy indulging in the weed.

As for the Dude's best friend, Walter Sobchak, he was an amalgam of at least two originals. One, according to William Preston Robertson's entertaining book on the making of the film, was the brothers' Uncle Peter, a bitter Vietnam veteran. Peter told the boys of having his rug stolen, saying that it had "tied the room together," a phrase that stayed with them, although somehow in the creative process the rug became the Dude's. Uncle Peter also told them about a friend, another vet, whose car was stolen by a kid who left his homework in it; this too found its way into the complicated plot of the film. The other influence on the character was the writer and director John Milius *(The Wind and the*

Lion, Red Dawn), whom they had met while making *Barton Fink*. A gun collector and survivalist, Milius had asked the boys to come up and see his gun collection, but they declined the offer.

The friendship of the Dude, Walter, and Donny (something of a foil for the other two) would make *The Big Lebowski* a kind of buddy picture. Male companionship was a frequently recurring theme in Joel and Ethan's films, from Hi and the Snopes brothers in *Raising Arizona* to Barton Fink and Charlie Meadows. In this case it wasn't prison or adjacent hotel rooms that bonded them together, but bowling. Again the basis was factual, for the brothers had known someone in L.A. — sometimes they said it was the original "Dude," sometimes their uncle — who played in a local amateur softball league. Joel said, "But we changed it to bowling because it was so much more visually compelling, and it's the kind of sport you can do when you're drinking and smoking. And it's also very retro, just as the characters seem to be from an earlier time." That male and female bowling leagues were separate meant that in the picture the bowling alley could become an enclosed little male society.

As always, other influences went into the mix. The character of Jackie Treehorn, wealthy pornographer, came from the suave night-club owners in Chandler's novels such as Norris in *The Big Sleep*, as well as from Hugh Hefner. The time period — the Gulf War of 1991 — did not, as usual, come from any burning interest in that moment in history. Instead, the brothers just wanted to give Walter something to rant about. Besides, it was better, they believed, to set every film in a specific moment rather than just the vague present.

And so, once again, the brothers began to write without an outline, throwing around ideas, pacing, wasting time, napping — and writing. Not working out the whole plot of a mystery in advance naturally led to some confusion. Sometimes they would imagine a surprising moment, such as the arrival of the severed toe, and then have to figure out its place in the story. "At a certain point," Ethan said, "we had to sit down and say, 'All right, it's gotta be *some*body's fucking toe.'" The story followed another typical Coen brothers pattern too; the poor hero had to undergo countless humiliations and maulings before hitting bottom.

With their fondness for narration, and their wanting to catch something of Chandler's novelistic voice, the brothers decided to frame the story with a voice-over. It wasn't really practical to make the Dude the narrator of his own story, and so they created a character who stood outside the plot and gave it a kind of fairy-tale quality. The Stranger, they called him, and so sure were they of the sort of comforting, authoritative western twang they wanted for the character that in the script they invoked the name of Sam Elliott, an actor who specialized in westerns. As to why the narrator should be a cowboy the brothers couldn't say; it was just one of their instinctive creative impulses at work, without any explicit symbolism behind it that they were aware of or particularly cared to think about. Perhaps it had something to do with the early frontier mentality of the west and the settling of California.

Joel and Ethan wanted to populate the movie with more characters than they had used before, to create a true Californian world of eccentrics and misfits. One that came up early was the friends' bowling rival, Jesus Quintana, the Hispanic pederast in a sleek jumpsuit. Joel had seen the actor John Turturro play a pederast in a Public Theater production in New York and lifted the idea for Jesus. The character of the rich Lebowski came from Chandler, but the wheelchair may well have been borrowed from the evil Mr. Potter in Capra's *It's a Wonderful Life*, an influence left over from *The Hudsucker Proxy*. Maude the artist was based on the real Fluxus movement of the 1960s which was more concerned with process than outcome. The brothers added dream sequences for the Dude — "a cheap, gimmicky, obvious way to depict the character's inner life," said Ethan — imagining them as Busby Berkeley musical numbers. Whatever they could throw into this shaggy-dog story, they did. Whatever seemed funny they kept in. Most of all, they had fun making their characters talk — fountains of testosterone-soaked rhetoric from Walter, good-natured if flaky cynicism from the Dude, perverse obscenities from Jesus, hardball capitalism from the rich Lebowski, and so on. And because it was a comedy, even Joel and Ethan knew that somehow it would turn out all right in the end.

The screenplay opens with the sound of a cowboy tune, "Tumbling Tumbleweeds," and a shot of a "steep, scrubby slope" rising to reveal the sprawling city of Los Angeles below. And as a voice sounding like Sam Elliott introduces him, we see the disheveled Dude himself, prowling an empty supermarket aisle before drinking from a carton of milk. Back at his apartment, in his bath, the Dude is suddenly hauled out by two men, and his head is plunged into the toilet. "Where's the fucking money, Lebowski?" they demand, while one of them urinates on the Dude's rug. But it turns out that they have mixed up two Jeff Lebowskis and are looking for a married

Male society: Jeff Bridges, John Goodman, and Steve Buscemi keep
score in *The Big Lebowski*   GLOBE PHOTOS

millionaire. "Hey, at least I'm housebroken," the Dude says in disgust.

A visual ballet of bowling images — flying pins, sliding feet — provides
background for the opening credits and the introduction of the Dude-Walter-
Donny friendship. Walter convinces the Dude that he ought to seek
compensation from the millionaire Jeff Lebowski for the rug that, as the Dude
laments, "really tied the room together." He goes to the Big Lebowski's mansion,
but although the thugs were trying to collect on debts accumulated by the rich
man, the blustery capitalist blows him off. "Your 'revolution' is over, Mr.
Lebowski," the big man says, dismissing the Dude's holdover sixties values. "The
bums lost." The Dude, however, takes a rug from the mansion anyway, meeting
on the way out a sexy young woman at the poolside — Bunny Lebowski. The
wife of the rich man offers to felate the Dude for a thousand dollars. "I'm just
gonna find a cash machine," says the Dude before being ushered out.

Another bowling alley scene allows Walter to show his war-vet temperament
as he pulls a gun on a fellow bowler. The Dude is called back to the mansion of
the Big Lebowski by his obsequious assistant Brandt, only to find out that Mrs.

Bunny Lebowski has been kidnapped. The millionaire wants to hire the Dude to act as courier for the ransom money. Back in the bowling alley, Dude tells his friends of the plan, speculating that Bunny actually kidnapped herself to get more money from her husband. Meanwhile, their bowling rival, the child-sex offender Jesus Quintana, tells the friends that he and his bowling partner are going to "fuck you up" in the league semifinals.

Walter accompanies Dude in the car to deliver the ransom, bringing a "ringer," a valise of unwashed underwear to throw out instead of the money. But the two argue and struggle in the car, Walter rolls from the car firing off a machine gun, and the kidnappers roar off on their motorcycles with the exchange never taking place. In the bowling alley, the Dude worries that the kidnappers will kill Bunny, while Walter rages about being scheduled for a semifinal bowling match on Saturday. "I don't roll on Shabbats" says Walter, a Jewish convert. Out in the parking lot, things go from bad to worse as the Dude discovers that his car has been stolen — along with the million-dollar ransom money.

The Dude's new rug is also gone, taken by the Big Lebowski's daughter, Maude, who asks him to visit. He finds the artist suspended naked in an overhead sling, dropping paint onto a canvas. Maude considers herself a radical feminist artist whose work is strongly "vaginal" and therefore threatening to men. She shows him a porno video starring none other than Bunny and offers him $100,000 if he can recover the ransom money. The Dude is just thinking that events are turning in his favor when he is hustled into a limousine and confronted by the Big Lebowski, who shows him a severed toe he has just received — presumably Bunny's, a warning from the kidnappers. Soaking in the tub again, he finds his apartment invaded by three German nihilists demanding the ransom money or else "Tomorrow ve come back and cut off your chonson." After visiting Maude again, who sends him to a doctor, Dude and Walter visit the boy who supposedly stole Dude's car, leaving his homework inside it. Thinking that the boy bought a new Corvette with the ransom money, Walter vandalizes the car with a baseball bat, only to discover it belongs to someone else.

The Dude is then picked up and brought to see Jackie Treehorn, millionaire pornographer, who wants the money owed to him by Bunny. Treehorn spikes Dude's drink, causing him to have a dream in the style of a Busby Berkeley musical, complete with chorus girls and Maude as a bowling ball–breasted Viking.

Back at his apartment, Dude finds Maude, who wants to have sex with Dude; he is puzzled but complies. Maude tells Dude that her father isn't rich at all but is merely using money from the family foundation, and also that she slept with him in order to conceive a child. Dude now believes that the Big Lebowski's bag of ransom money was empty and that he planned to keep the foundation's million dollars for himself. He and Walter go to the mansion, only to find a naked Bunny jumping into the pool, never having been kidnapped at all. Now they confront the Big Lebowski on the whereabouts of the million and Walter, believing (wrongly, as it turns out) that the man isn't really handicapped, dumps him out of his wheelchair.

Outside the bowling alley, Dude, Walter, and Donny are confronted by the three nihilists. A comic fight ensues, during which Donny has a heart attack. The scene cuts to the mortuary where Walter and Dude are choosing a coffin for their dead comrade. Taking Donny's remains in a coffee can to a high bluff, Walter tosses the ashes, only to have them blow all over the Dude. "Awww, fuck it, Dude," says Walter. "Let's go bowling." And they do. In the final scene the Dude is at the bowling alley bar as the Stranger sidles up next to him. They talk and then the Stranger gives his final speech to the camera. "Welp, that about does her, wraps her all up," he says. "Made me laugh to beat the band. Parts, anyway."

It was not Joel and Ethan's most profound script, but it was the most convoluted, and perhaps the funniest.

The Romance of Bowling

With the script ready, it was a simple matter to go into preproduction as soon as *Fargo* wrapped. Once again PolyGram and Working Title put up the budget — $15 million this time, almost two and a half times that of *Fargo*, but still hardly astronomical by Hollywood standards. Once more Roger Deakins would be cinematographer, while production designer Rick Heinrichs and costume designer Mary Zophres would both head their departments for the second time. Using Ethan's thumbnail sketches made while talking through the scenes, the brothers, along with artist J. Todd Anderson and Deakins, worked through the storyboards. This took more effort than for *Fargo* as Joel wanted to give the picture a more overt and frankly showy visual style. A lot of time was spent talking about the bowling alley scenes and "Brunswick styling," a reference to the Brunswick company's classic 1950s decorative style used in many alleys. Joel saw the lanes, pins, gutters, and moving balls as opportunities for some artful painting with movement, color, and lines. The other settings, too, would allow for a rich palette of California colors, in marked contrast to the subdued look of the last few films. If the dominant color of *Fargo* was white, *The Hudsucker Proxy* silver, and *Barton Fink* bile-green, then *The Big Lebowski* would be a whole range of California pastels.

Jeff Bridges had already agreed to be the Dude, a part which, in retrospect, he seemed born to play. A son, along with brother Beau, of the late actor Lloyd Bridges, Jeff had made his film debut at the age of four months. By eight he was a regular in his father's television series, *Sea Hunt*, but unlike so many child actors his appeal did not end with adolescence. At the age of 22, he earned an Academy Award nomination for Peter Bogdanovich's *The Last Picture Show*, and he has since gone on to act in hundreds of films. His career has had its shares of highs and lows, as has his personal life, although he eventually cleared the drugs out of his system and settled down. He had just given some of his most memorable performances in such films as *Tucker: A Man and His Dream*, *The Fabulous Baker Boys*, *The Fisher King*, and *Fearless*. He had developed what appeared to be an almost effortless yet totally convincing acting style, and he projected a charismatic but unglamorous image that seemed more real and more human than that of most leading actors.

The brothers also knew that they wanted John Goodman to play Walter. His large, blustering, comic quality, laced with a darker undertone, was just what was needed to bring the Vietnam vet and converted Jew ("I'm as Jewish as fucking Tevye") to life. Waiting for Bridges' schedule to open up worked fine for Goodman, who had also been too busy taping *Roseanne*. This would be his third film for the brothers. Three other regulars would join the cast. Steve Buscemi would be Donny, the guy always trying to keep up with his brighter friends' conversation. John Turturro would become Jesus, a comic role that the intense actor could immerse himself in, transforming his voice and his body. Instead of being alienated from his physical self as he was as *Barton Fink*, he would become highly, even excessively aware of his sexualized nature. And Peter Stormare and Jon Polito would have small roles, the former as one of the trio of nihilists (really a comic take on his murderous character in *Fargo*), the latter as a private eye.

Julianne Moore was cast as Maude, the Big Lebowski's artist daughter. An "army brat" who had grown up in 23 different places, Moore began acting in off-Broadway theater, played twin sisters in the television soap *As the World Turns*, and had gone on to movies. Tara Reid, a young actress who had appeared in her first film just the year before, was picked for the Big Lebowski's very young, sexually wayward wife. Ben Gazzara, perhaps most noteworthy for his roles in John Cassavetes movies and now in semiretirement, was induced to play the smooth Jackie Treehorn. And who better to play the Stranger, the cowboy narrator with a voice like Sam Elliott, than Sam Elliott himself?

Joel and Ethan told Rick Heinrichs, who had been the production designer on *Fargo*, that they wanted a bright, glowing, surreal look for the film. Heinrichs used a lot of Los Angeles style books for reference. For Jackie Treehorn's wild party the brothers casually mentioned that it ought to have an "Inca" theme, sending him to the library once more. At least he didn't have to construct a bowling alley — the real Hollywood Star Lanes had been chosen as a location site. He did have it repainted — using colors the owner agreed to so that they wouldn't have to paint it back again — and added neon stars to the outside wall, visually connecting it to the starry backdrops of the Dude's dream sequences.

Mary Zophres, who also worked on *Fargo*, began assembling the costumes, going for a more realistic than stylized look. Her first fitting with Jeff Bridges lasted two hours as he tried on two racks of clothes. More fittings followed; fortunately Bridges enjoyed finding the right look for his character, in this case a low-rent beachwear style, in keeping with the Dude's Venice Beach neighborhood. She wanted him to wear flip-flops, but Bridges, who has a bad back, didn't think he could work all day in them. They settled for plastic beach shoes instead. For Goodman's Walter Sobchak she came up with a "suburbanized" military look that went with his "Norman Schwarzkopf" haircut. Both actors' wardrobes had to be stressed and aged to make it seem as if these were real people's clothes.

Just Dropped In

Despite the hoopla over the Academy Awards, shooting went smoothly. Jeff

Joel and Ethan are characteristically calm on the set of *The Big Lebowski*   FOTOS INTERNATIONAL/ARCHIVE PHOTOS

Bridges found the brothers very relaxed, never arguing on the set. If they did have a disagreement, Joel shot the scene both ways for the matter to be settled later in the editing room. Julianne Moore too found it a casual shoot; "They don't really talk a lot, which I love," she said.

Nevertheless, the shoot was complicated by the many stylish shots that Joel wanted. As well, there were more locations than usual for a Coen brothers film and real locations always provide limitations in camera movement and lighting that must be worked around. The cinematographer and his crew have to be on their toes to make sure there is a uniform look to all their shots. Not only were there many locations, but many night shots too. Deakins bathed them in an orange glow, which the photo lab kept trying to "correct" until they were told not to.

One night shot that was supposed to go without a hitch ended up holding up shooting for hours. John Goodman was supposed to hurl the bag of ransom money (actually the ringer bag of underwear) out of the moving car's window in a high arc. But no matter what he did, the bag just plopped to the ground.

Nor could a stunt double do better. Tying a nylon line to the bag and pulling it only looked ridiculous. Finally Jeff Bridges came up with the solution: to shoot the moment backwards by having someone hurl the bag into the air and down to the car window, then reverse the shot for the film. The brothers had done similar reverse shots on *Raising Arizona* but hadn't thought of it here. It worked.

One of the bigger challenges of the film was the Busby Berkeley–style dance sequence taking place within the Dude's dream after he's been drugged by Jackie Treehorn. Although Berkeley's musical numbers are now considered kitsch by most, the brothers professed to view him as a hero. And it is not hard to see why Joel in particular would have appreciated his innovative camera movements, creating dances that could only exist on film because the camera's viewpoint — from overhead, for instance — could never otherwise be seen by an audience. As well, the brothers enjoyed the fact that Berkeley felt no need to connect the dance numbers to the film's story. And if those glossy dances, with their lines of leggy females in perfect synchronization, did look a bit cheesy — well, that was just another reason to like them!

Joel wanted their own version, shot in a converted airplane hangar, to look just as showy and expensive as a 1940s MGM musical, even if it was modest compared to some of Berkeley's work. From the beginning they knew the soundtrack would be Kenny Rogers' song "Just Dropped In." (Music — not just the original score but the use of popular songs from the sixties on — is perhaps more important and integral to the Coens' conception of scenes than I have so far explored. No doubt at this very moment someone is writing a PhD thesis on *Pop Music as Ironic Counterpoint to the Themes of the Coen Brothers.*) The opening shot of the Dude appearing as a tiny figure boogying against a colossal wall was actually Rick Heinrich's idea. The part where the Dude floats horizontally between the legs of the chorus girls with their arms spread wide required two matched sets of film. The first had Jeff lying horizontal and rotating in a harness. The second had the women against a blue screen; very tall dancers had to be chosen in order for Bridges' image to fit through their legs. For cutting to the Dude's point of view they used the simple technique of mounting the camera on a pole and pushing it along the leggy aisle. After it was all over, Joel and Ethan had even more admiration for Berkeley than when they had started.

The cast of *The Big Lebowski* with Ethan at the premiere party, just the sort of event the brothers dislike   WALTER WEISSMAN/GLOBE PHOTOS

No more time for dumb questions: John Goodman with the Coens at a press conference for *The Big Lebowski*

HANS EDINGER/AP PHOTO

A Lesson for America?

Postproduction on the film was naturally more complicated than for *Fargo*. The brothers still edited it themselves, however, along with Ethan's wife Tricia Cooke, who for the first time was given equal editing credit. After the success of *Fargo*, there was a sense of anticipation over the next Coen brothers film that went beyond their core legion of loyal fans. Had they truly become filmmakers with a mainstream audience?

The reviews duly came out and they were, well, pretty good or not bad, depending on your point of view. Janet Maslin of the *New York Times* picked up the film's mood nicely, calling it "loopier" than *Fargo*, "a mode in which their actors are supremely comfortable." She didn't mind a plot that "need not be taken too seriously" and praised Jeff Bridges for "a role so right for him that he seems never to have been anywhere else." And she ended her review in just the same way as countless other critics, by agreeing with the voice of the Stranger who ends the film by saying, "Made me laugh to beat the band. Parts, anyway."

Most reviewers noted the film's humor and easy charm and the supremely likable main characters — and also the meandering plot with its tendency to sprawl rather than deepen. The *New York Post* critic thought the film lost its way but still praised Bridges' great performance and the comedy. Many reviewers told their readers that if they didn't take the film too seriously they would find it a lot of fun. Probably the Coens would have agreed. One of the most insightful commentaries came from Jonathan Romney in *Sight and Sound*, admittedly not a journal read by the average moviegoer. He did not complain of the loose plot but celebrated it. He also noted that despite it being a quasi-detective film it contained no real evil. The Dude was "laudable not for his moral integrity as such, but because deep ingrained inertia makes him impervious to corruption." For this reason the Dude had no need of being redeemed or even changed, breaking a cardinal rule of most mainstream films.

None of the more negative reviews were outright pans or attacks as some of the previous films had received. *Variety* wrote that the film had "wonderfully funny sequences and some brilliantly original notions," but that it added up to "considerably less than the sum of its scintillating parts, simply because the film doesn't seem to be about anything other than its own cleverness." Richard Schickel in *Time* called the story "incomprehensible" and the film-noir refer-

ences a bit stale, but he praised John Goodman and still found the plot fascinating at times. While Kenneth Turan of the *Los Angeles Times* found the story
"disjointed, incoherent, and even irritating," he had to admit the brothers wrote
parts that actors thrived in.

In the end, the reviewers couldn't help admitting that the film was no *Fargo*.
Of course — it was never meant to be. To say that it was about nothing, as a few
asserted, didn't seem fair or accurate; at the very least it was about two very particular characters, the Dude and Walter, and their very different approaches to
life. The early bowling scenes were filmed with particular elan — they alone
made the film worth watching. If it was true that the film seemed to wander too
much in its later half, losing its focus on the characters as the action became
more frenetic, this trait was characteristic of all the brothers' films, even *Fargo*.
But all in all, critics were more balanced in their judgments than they had been
with some of the brothers' earlier efforts. *The Big Lebowski*, they concluded, was
an easy picture to enjoy, but perhaps it was not as memorable as earlier films by
the brothers, even those which were not always liked as much. *Barton Fink*, for
example, was a much harder film to "like" but also a harder one to forget.

During the press tour to promote the film the brothers seemed a little surly.
Asked about their philosophy of filmmaking, Ethan replied, "Oooh — I don't
have one. I wouldn't even know how to begin. You've stumped me there. None
that I've noticed. Drawing a blank on this one." (One wonders if the answer
would have been different if the question had come from a French intellectual
film journal.) In answer to a question about whether they were trying to teach
Americans the meaning of nihilism, Ethan replied in a sarcastic tone:
"Everything's a lesson for America." Perhaps he was just becoming ever more
bored of interviews, which neither of the brothers had ever liked. Or perhaps he
was annoyed by the film's lack of success; it took in only $10 million dollars at
American theaters, a third less than its production budget and a substantial
drop from *Fargo*'s $25 million. The larger audience had not returned to see
what the two talented brothers might be up to next. America, it seemed, preferred any dumbed-down comedy or tired action picture to the Coens'
originality and verve. Surely this had to hurt, even for filmmakers as outwardly
uncaring of success as Joel and Ethan. For all intents and purposes, they were
again indie filmmakers, who happened to have big-studio backing. On the
other hand, this was a lesson that virtually every original filmmaker in America

has had to learn, from Steven Soderbergh to Hal Hartley, and even including such famous directors as Woody Allen and Martin Scorsese, both of whom have made many acclaimed films without ever having a truly big hit. Perhaps Joel and Ethan should have followed the example of their friend Sam *"Evil Dead"* Raimi and made *Fargo II: The Woodchipper's Revenge.* The audience might have returned for that. But repeating themselves would have just bored the brothers.

As Marge says to her suspect handcuffed in the backseat of her cruiser, "There's more to life than a little money, you know."

CHAPTER TEN

ETHAN COEN, AUTHOR

"We are none of us perfect; I know that."
— Ethan Canin, *The Gates of Eden*

From childhood it was always Ethan who loved reading the most. He was one of those kids who always had to be carrying a book around with him. He began writing early; Joel was likely the first to recognize his younger brother's talent, and eventually saw how useful it could be to him in his desire to make movies. It was Joel who brought Ethan into film, talking up the idea of writing an independent feature together even before Ethan graduated from Princeton. And while the two have been genuine collaborators ever since, taking equal responsibility for their screenplays and simply changing the order of their names in the credits at whim, it is tempting to speculate that while Joel has the greater ability to see a film in visual terms, Ethan may be the real genius behind the inventive, witty, disturbing dialogue.

While Joel never wanted to write anything besides movies,

A subdued Ethan Coen
at *The Big Lebowski*
premiere
SONIA MOSKOWITZ/
GLOBE PHOTOS

Ethan's interest has always been broader. For example, a play he wrote, called *Mammon and Fist*, was performed in the new play series of the American Conservatory Theatre, a professional regional theater in San Francisco. It is also interesting to wonder whether Ethan, despite getting along so well with Joel, has sometimes hungered after an artistic identity of his own. After all, Joel is always the brother mentioned first (as in "Joel and Ethan Coen"), as if Ethan were tagging behind. In filmmaking, it is the director who is often considered the true "auteur" and Joel often gets the credit — and award nominations — for the splendid look of the films. No one, on the other hand, pats Ethan on the back for being named the producer.

There is no need to exaggerate this point; the brothers seem to be remarkably free of sibling rivalry. And the obvious truth is that each helps to fulfill the other's artistic talent. But that is not to say that Ethan hasn't had a hankering to be a "real" author with his name on the cover of a book. And so it is not surprising that, taking a step towards autonomy, Ethan began writing short stories. And he began publishing them too — in *Playboy*, *Vanity Fair*, and even eventually the *New Yorker*, the most prestigious magazine in which to publish short stories in America.

It probably didn't hurt that Ethan already had a reputation as a hip film-maker; by publishing his fiction, the magazines might hope to attract curious readers. But all three magazines had very high standards and were unlikely to lower them when they could get work from virtually any writer in the country. And it is easy to see why Ethan's fiction appealed to editor Rob Weisbach, who had his own imprint at William Morrow & Co. and won the right to publish Ethan's stories as the collection *Gates of Eden*. Weisbach not only had discerning tastes, but a liking for young, edgy fiction that cut through traditional boundaries.

Anyone reading Ethan's stories would have no trouble identifying him as the co-author of the Coen brothers' screenplays. Funny before everything else, they usually work by making comic hay out of classic genre situations. Probably best is the first story in the collection, "Destiny," about a middle-class kid turned boxer — or rather, punching bag. The young boxer, in contrast to the gangster characters in the story, is well-spoken and polite, as if nice, middle-class Ethan himself were a character somehow dropped among the eccentrics and killers of his own films. Its energy comes from the juxtaposition of these two worlds:

> *". . . That's good, kid. You got a sense a humor; that'll see you through the low points. And you're educated; just listen to ya talk, just listen to ya, will ya? What did I tell ya, kid? Did I tell ya fighting is a mental game? Being mentally on the ball — you got that. You got a leg up there on these other bums. A good leg. Now this fight — "*
> *"This beating."*
> *"Heh-heh. This fight — "*
> *"No no, really. It was a beating."*
> *"Heh-heh. Okay, this beaten, kid. You know what the problem was?"*
> *"Tell me."*
> *"You were thinkin' too much."*

The story's narrative elements — adultery, secret photos — are reminiscent of *Blood Simple* minus the gore. The dark side of the films is not much in evidence here; instead, the humor tells the reader not to take the situation too seriously.

One fascinating story, "The Old Country," may provide a glimpse (if in comic form again) of the brothers' suburban Jewish upbringing. Reminiscent of early Philip Roth, it tells the story of a kid who rebels in Hebrew school. Written from the viewpoint of a sensitive narrator, it allowed Ethan to write in the kind of first-person coming-of-age voice that cannot be reproduced easily in film:

> *Michael Simkin's family was rich. This was common knowledge, in the way that it is among children. There was even a rumor, never substantiated, that the Simkins had a bowling alley in their basement, a rich person's solitary lane with Brunswick pin-setting and below-ground ball return. To us his parents' wealth was neither here nor there except during the tree drive. We were all encouraged to bring in money to be used to plant trees in the state of Israel, in support of her effort to make the desert bloom. For each tree endowed a student received a printed certificate bearing the signature of Levi Eshkol and the words "'And when ye shall come into the land and ye shall plant . . .' Leviticus 19:23." Michael had a dozen certificates, all of which he threw into the snack hall ceiling, and also a medallion for having planted ten or more trees, which he threw out the window of the Hebrew school bus at a pursuing dog.*

Bowling alley aside, this was not the kind of material that the brothers drew on for their films. Most of the other stories were straight dialogue, like miniature film scripts. There is a lot of detective fiction, or rather film-noir parody. In other words, aside from some notable exceptions, Ethan's first collection of stories didn't stray too far from the subject matter or the form that he was most familiar with.

Published in November, 1998, eight months after the release of *The Big Lebowski, Gates of Eden* was well received by book critics, who might have been expected to approach a screenplay author turned fiction writer with skepticism. In the *New York Times* Christopher Lehman-Haupt called the stories ". . . often funny, sometimes disturbing," and noted the contrast between the growing-up-Jewish-in-Minnesota stories and the more violent works. Wondering aloud where the violent images came from, he concluded that their source was the confusion of identity and loss of purpose which modern American Jews suffer. Ethan, he concluded, had imaginatively transformed these feelings into images of adultery and murder. It was an intriguing solution, if perhaps too neat and simple.

MORE MOVIES, BIGGER CAMERAS

"Heck, we're doin' pretty good, Norm."
— Marge in *Fargo*

Joel and Ethan's approach to their career is relatively simple; as soon as they wrap one movie they start another. Quite often a new script is already finished and ready to go into preproduction. Aside from spending time with their families, making movies is about all they do or want to do.

After *The Big Lebowski* the brothers had not one but several projects in progress at the same time. One — the one to be released first — is called *Oh Brother, Where Art Thou?* This is a rather esoteric joke, coming as it does from the brothers' favorite Preston Sturges film, *Sullivan's Travels*. In Sturges' film a Hollywood director of silly entertainments decides to make a serious film about the Depression called by the same name. But because he actually knows only wealth and success, he decides to disguise himself as a hobo and go on the road, eventually ending up in prison. The lesson that the director learns while watching the prisoners laughing uproariously at a

An insider's joke for Preston Sturges fans: George Clooney and Holly Hunter at the Cannes Film Festival for the screening of *O Brother, Where Art Thou?*

MICHEL EVLER/AP PHOTO

church screening of cartoons is that audiences don't want to see their lives depicted in movies; they want to escape for a little while. It is not yet clear how Joel and Ethan's film relates to *Sullivan's Travel*, although it does have George Clooney, the ER heartthrob turned big-screen actor, as a 1930s convict leading a chain gang who escape and have to keep a tracker off their trail while looking for buried loot. It also sounds reminiscent of a 1955 Humphrey Bogart picture called *We're No Angels*. John Goodman, returning for his fourth Coen brothers film, plays the bad guy in the guise of a bible salesman. To confuse matters, the brothers claim that their story was based on Homer's *Odyssey*. The film is a coproduction of Universal and Disney, both new studios for the brothers.

The other three projects that the Coen brothers have underway are all a break from their usual working methods. Until now, they have refused to work as hired guns on anyone else's picture, or to write adaptations or screenplays for anyone but themselves. However, Joel and Ethan agreed to adapt a new Elmore Leonard novel, *Cuba Libre*, before it even came out, for Universal and the producers Brillstein-Grey. It is the first time they have ever been hired by others, but it is easy to see why the project would appeal to them. The primary reason would be that Elmore Leonard is no doubt an author they admire. The secondary reason might be that Leonard novels such as *Get Shorty* have adapted well to the screen. The third might be that at this point in their lives, the brothers don't feel that making a little (or a lot of) money on the side will damage their integrity or sidetrack their careers. While the producers would like Joel to direct the film, he is reported to be uncommitted.

Yet another adaptation the brothers have penned is a screenplay based on *To the White Sea*, a novel by the late James Dickey, best known as the author of *Deliverance*. The novel is a World War II story about a B29 gunner named Muldrow shot down while on a bombing mission over Tokyo. Formerly an Alaskan hunter, Muldrow must use his survival skills to stay alive. Reports have it that the only dialogue in the screenplay takes place in the first five minutes. The film was supposed to be shot before *Cuba Libre*, but didn't get the studio OK in time.

A project that sounds purely like a moneymaker is a screenplay called *Intolerable Cruelty*. Although written by Joel and Ethan, the brothers do not plan to be involved in the making of it. Richard Gere is set to star as a philandering Beverly Hills lawyer who gets married to a woman who, unknown to him, wants to take revenge on him.

Turn around, boys: George Clooney, Tim Blake Nelson, and John Turturro at Cannes for *O Brother, Where Art Thou?*   MICHEL EVLER/AP PHOTO

Joel Coen once said that the only real difference between the filmmaking that he and his brother do now and the Super-8 films they made as kids was "bigger cameras." Within that joke is a genuine truth that all artists know — the same imaginative impulse they felt as children guides them even as adults.

The need to invent, to tell stories, to find a way to depict or even refashion the world — these impulses were there from an early age for Joel and Ethan. No doubt their gentle if bland suburban upbringing was a kind of blank canvas waiting to have a more interesting image cast upon it. Their early television watching — movies, cartoons, and other small-screen fodder — must have provided them with some of the basic character types, narrative strategies, and genre styles for their own later works. Their imaginations were further stoked by the reading of high and low literature, of philosophy (in Ethan's case) with its questions about existence, alienation, and truth, and with a discovery (in Joel's case) of "artistic films" (Polanski, Kurosawa). Even their first experience in filmmaking — those low-budget horror movies of Sam Raimi and others — went into the mix.

But what has come out is pure Coen brothers. There may or may not be a "Barton Fink feeling" but there is definitely a Coen brothers feeling. For one thing, almost every one of their films leaves the viewer feeling distinctly uneasy; the exception is *The Big Lebowski*, but there is always an exception when one is trying to generalize about the Coens. They are all, in a sense, horror films. Even the comic *Raising Arizona* has a nightmarish quality, and the hero and heroine may have had their lives ruined by their own uncontrollable impulses. Despite being their most satisfying film next to *Fargo*, *Miller's Crossing* may leave us with an uncomfortable feeling that we are somehow being fooled into taking these tragic characters at face value. And then there is *Barton Fink*, the most truly horrific of their films and arguably the most intellectually provocative. Is it not Barton's monstrous artistic ego that somehow releases the murderous Karl Mundt into the world?

As for *The Hudsucker Proxy*, its horror may or may not be intentional, but beneath that glittering style is a frightening void, a black hole of meaninglessness that calls the whole complicated and expensive filmmaking exercise into question. A lot of sound and fury signifying nothing? After that came the praised, loved, much-awarded *Fargo*, the first Coen brothers film we could really love. It begins with a state trooper and two innocent passersby being murdered in cold blood. It goes on to the "comic" kidnapping of a terrified housewife, who later ends up dead, still bound to a chair. Her loving father dies too, as does another innocent bystander. Then one of the bad guys, after having half his face shot off, is himself murdered and his body shredded. But we can love the film because the remaining bad guy gets arrested by the pregnant cop who loves her husband and talks in a quaint Minnesotan accent. For a moment we half forget that the cop's baby will be born into a world whose evil most of us simply cannot comprehend.

After all that horror, *The Big Lebowski* ought to come as something of a relief. Sure, there's a supposed kidnapping. And someone's toe gets cut off. And a rich, frustrated old man in a wheelchair is held in emotional torment by a young wife. And a convicted pederast offers obscenities. And a Vietnam vet is such a caldron of frustration and anger that he pulls a gun on a guy in a bowling alley. And a pothead who just wants to be left alone gets beaten up more times than most of us can keep track of. But it's a comedy, and it really is funny, and perhaps we don't take all of this too seriously. And maybe the Dude is the most likable of any Coen brothers character (unless you prefer Marge) because of his Zen-like approach to life. In "Storybuilding 101" the first thing you learn is that your character has to *want* something, but the Dude wants nothing but to be left alone. And we agree — the rug really *did* tie the room together.

At the end of *The Big Lebowski* the Dude finds himself talking to the Stranger at the bar in the bowling alley. The Stranger asks him how things have been going. The Dude replies: "Ahh, you know. Strikes and gutters, ups and downs." It is a fair enough assessment, although most of us don't usually accept it with such equanimity. The Coen brothers seem to, however, at least when it comes to their own careers in filmmaking. Perhaps bowling isn't the best metaphor for artistic endeavor, but what the hell. The Coens keep throwing those balls, with greater or lesser accuracy, but somehow or other the pins always fall down in an interesting way. Studio-backed or not, Joel and Ethan are true independent filmmakers. They make their own films their own way, following their own skewed vision. And those of us who care about movies will keep watching with fascination, horror, and surprise. And laughter, too — most of the time, anyway.

A COEN BROTHERS FILMOGRAPHY

Blood Simple

1985

Directed by Joel Coen

Produced by Ethan Coen

Screenplay by Joel Coen and Ethan Coen

A Circle Releasing Corporation Release

Featuring John Getz, Frances McDormand, Dan Hedaya, Samm-Art Williams, M. Emmet Walsh

Crimewave

AKA *The XYZ Murders, Broken Hearts and Noses*

1985

Directed by Sam Raimi

Produced by Robert Tapert

Screenplay by Ethan Coen, Joel Coen, and Sam Raimi

A Columbia Pictures Release

Featuring Louise Lasser, Edward R. Pressman, Paul L. Smith, Brion James, Sheree J. Wilson, Bruce Campbell, Reed Birney, Hamid Dana

Raising Arizona
1987
Directed by Joel Coen
Produced by Ethan Coen
Screenplay by Ethan Coen and Joel Coen
A Twentieth Century Fox Release
Featuring Nicolas Cage, Holly Hunter, Trey Wilson, John Goodman, William Forsythe, Sam McMurray, Frances McDormand, Randall (Tex) Cobb, T.J. Kuhn, Lynne Dumin Kitei

Miller's Crossing
1990
Directed by Joel Coen
Produced by Ethan Coen
Screenplay by Joel Coen and Ethan Coen
A Twentieth Century Fox Release
Featuring Gabriel Byrne, Albert Finney, Marcia Gay Harden, Jon Polito, John Turturro, J.E. Freeman, Steve Buscemi

Barton Fink
1991
Directed by Joel Coen
Produced by Ethan Coen
Screenplay by Ethan Coen and Joel Coen
A Twentieth Century Fox Release
Featuring John Turturro, John Goodman, Judy Davis, Michael Lerner, John Mahoney, Jon Polito, Tony Shalhoub

The Hudsucker Proxy
1994
Directed by Joel Coen
Produced by Ethan Coen

Screenplay by Ethan Coen, Joel Coen, and Sam Raimi

A Warner Brothers Release

Featuring Tim Robbins, Jennifer Jason Leigh, Paul Newman, Charles Durning, John Mahoney

Fargo

1996

Directed by Joel Coen

Produced by Ethan Coen

Screenplay by Joel Coen and Ethan Coen

A Gramercy Pictures Release

Featuring Frances McDormand, William H. Macy, Steve Buscemi, Peter Stormare, Harve Presnell, John Carroll Lynch, Kristin Rudrud

The Big Lebowski

1998

Directed by Joel Coen

Produced by Ethan Coen

Screenplay by Joel Coen and Ethan Coen

A Gramercy Pictures Release

Featuring Jeff Bridges, John Goodman, Steve Buscemi, John Turturro, Julianne Moore

O Brother, Where Art Thou?

2000

Directed by Joel Coen

Produced by Ethan Coen

Screenplay by Joel Coen and Ethan Coen

A Buena Vista Pictures Release

Featuring George Clooney, John Goodman, John Turturro, Holly Hunter, Tim Blake Nelson, Charles Durning, Mike Badalucco

BOOKS BY AND ABOUT THE COEN BROTHERS

Coen, Joel and Ethan Coen. *Blood Simple.* New York: St. Martin's Press, 1988.

Coen, Joel and Ethan Coen. *Raising Arizona.* New York: St Martin's Press, 1988.

Coen, Joel and Ethan Coen. *Barton Fink & Miller's Crossing.* London: Faber & Faber, 1991.

Coen, Joel, Ethan Coen, and Sam Raimi. *The Hudsucker Proxy.* London: Faber & Faber, 1994.

Coen, Ethan and Joel Coen. *Fargo.* London: Faber & Faber, 1996.

Coen, Ethan and Joel Coen. *The Big Lebowski.* London: Faber & Faber, 1998.

Cooke, Tricia, editor, and William Preston Robertson, text. *The Big Lebowski: The Making of a Coen Brothers Film.* New York: W.W. Norton, 1998.

Coen, Ethan. *Gates of Eden.* New York: William Morrow, 1998.

SOURCES

Chapter One

Eric Pooley, "Warped in America." *New York* March 23, 1987; *Crimewave* promotion kit; Barry Sonnenfeld, "Shadows and Shivers for *Blood Simple.*" *American Cinematographer* July 1985; Eric Breitbart, "Leaving the Seventies Behind, Four New York Independents Find Happiness Making Movies in the Manner of Hollywood." *American Film* April 1985; David Handleman, "The Brothers From Another Planet." *Rolling Stone* May 21, 1987; John H. Richardson, "The Joel and Ethan Story." *Premiere* Oct. 1990; Richard Harrington, "Two-Scoop Coen." *Kitchener-Waterloo Record* Nov. 1, 1990; Joan Goodman, "Behind the Scenes of a Masterful Double Bill." *Globe and Mail* Oct. 5, 1990; Bruce Kirkland, "Wicked Ways." *Marquee* Aug. 1991; Robert Seidenberg, "*Miller's Crossing.*" *American Film* vol. 15, no. 6; David Giammarco, "The Horror, the Horror of Sam Raimi." *Eye* Feb. 4, 1993; Owen Gleiberman, "Lord of the Ring." *Entertainment Weekly* March 11, 1994; "Coen, Joel." *Current Biography Yearbook*, edited by Judith Graham, H.W. Wilson, 1994; Ron Base, "Lessons in the Simple Art of (Movie) Murder." *Toronto Star* April 4, 1985; John Harkness, "Simple Brothers Sample Success." *Now* April 4, 1985; St. Louis Park, Minnesota, official web site; *The Hudsucker Proxy* promotion kit; Judy Klemesrud, "The Brothers Coen Bow in with *Blood Simple*." *New York Times* Jan. 29, 1985; Jay Scott, "New Yorkers Thirst for Coens' Blood." *Globe and Mail* March 8, 1995; Ethan Coen, *Gates of Eden*. William Morrow, 1998; Stephen Schiff, "Raising Coen." *Vanity Fair* April 1987; Leonard Klady, "Wacky Movie's Sibling Producers Hit on Hot Formula." *Toronto Star*; "The Most Original Horror Film of the Year Hits U.S. Screens." *Globe and Mail* April 16, 1983; David Ansen, "Mixing Blood and Chuckles." *Newsweek* Jan. 21, 1985; David Gritten, "The Coen Mystique." *Los Angeles Times* March 5, 1998; *Fargo* promotion kit; Dan Yakir, "Two Nice Boys and a Camera." *Globe and Mail* March 22, 1996; William Preston Robertson, "The Coen Brothers Made Easy." *Playboy* April 1994; Nick Roddick, "Oh Baby!" *Screen International* May 9, 1987; Hal Hinson, "Bloodlines." *Film Comment* March–April 1985; Simon's Rock of Bard College official web site; Har., "The Evil Dead." *Variety* February 9, 1983; Henry Mietkiewitz, "*The Evil Dead* an Energetic Curiosity Item." *Toronto Star* May 29, 1983; Vincent Canby, "If You Want to Make Movies, Learn To Be a Salesman." *New York Times* April 24, 1983; "Sam Raimi." *The Film Encyclopedia*, edited by Ephraim Katz, HarperCollins, 1998; 28th London Film Festival program notes.

Chapter Two

Nick Roddick, "Oh Baby!"; John Harkness, "*Raising Arizona*'s Content-Free Form." *Now* March 11, 1987; Hal Hinson, "Bloodlines"; Judy Klemesrud, "The Brothers Coen Bow in with *Blood Simple*"; John Clark, "Strange Bedfellows." *Premiere* April 1994; *Blood Simple* promotion kit; Peter Biskind, "Joel and Ethan Coen." *Premiere* March 1996; Eric Pooley, "Warped in America"; "Do Not Miss *Fargo*." *Interview* March 1996; Ron Base, "Lessons in the Simple Art of (Movie) Murder"; "Coen, Joel." *Current Biography Yearbook*; John H. Richardson, "The Joel and Ethan Story"; Joel Coen and Ethan Coen, *Blood Simple*. St. Martin's

Press, 1988; *Miller's Crossing* promotion kit; *Crimewave* promotion kit; Barry Sonnenfeld, "Shadows and Shivers for *Blood Simple*"; Eric Breitbart, "Leaving the Seventies Behind, Four New York Independents Find Happiness Making Movies in the Manner of Hollywood"; "Sonnenfeld, Barry." *The Film Encyclopedia*; Rick Lyman, "Through the Past, Slyly." *Globe and Mail* July 19, 1997; Jay Scott, "A Brilliant Descent Into the Depths." *Globe and Mail* Sept. 27, 1990; *Mr Showbiz* web site; Tricia Cooke, editor, William Preston Robertson, text, *The Big Lebowski: The Making of a Coen Brothers Film.* W.W. Norton, 1998; *Raising Arizona* promotion kit; *Blood Simple* promotion kit; Rick Lyman, "Marge's Other Job, You Betcha." *New York Times* Oct. 11, 1997; Rebecca Ascher-Walsh, "Queen Fargo." *Entertainment Weekly* April 12, 1996; *Raising Arizona* promotion kit; Jay Scott, "New Yorkers Thirst for Coens' *Blood*"; Tad Friend, "Inside the Coen Heads." *Vogue* April 1994; David Handelman, "The Brothers From Another Planet"; James Greenberg, "Low-Budget Thriller Aims For Both Art, Mass Auds." *Variety* July 5, 1985; Richard Harrington, "Two-Scoop Coen"; Robert Seidenberg, *"Miller's Crossing"*; William Preston Robertson, "The Coen Brothers Made Easy"; *Barton Fink* promotion kit; John Harkness, "Simple Brothers Sample Success"; Kenneth M. Chanko, "Ben Barenholtz." *Films in Review* Aug.–Sept. 1990; Stephen Schiff, "Raising Coen"; Silv., "*Blood Simple.*" *Variety* May 23, 1984; David Denby, "Where the Coyotes Howl." *New York* Jan. 21, 1985; Janet Maslin, "*Blood Simple* a Black Comic Romp." *New York Times* Oct. 12, 1984; David Ansen, "Mixing Blood and Chuckles." *Newsweek* Jan. 21, 1985; John Bloom, "*Blood Simple.*" *Dallas Times Herald* March 26, 1984; Richard Corliss, "Same Old Song." *Time* Jan. 28, 1985; Sheila Benson, "2 Movies: When a Bill of Fair Is a Bill of Goods." *Los Angeles Times* May 5, 1985; Pauline Kael. *New Yorker* Feb. 25, 1985; J. Hoberman, "The Glitz, the Drab, and the Baffling." *Village Voice* Jan. 22, 1985; John Powers, "Finking It." *Sight and Sound* Sept. 1991; David Ansen, "The Coens: Partners in Crime."

Chapter Three

John H. Richardson, "The Joel and Ethan Story"; *The Hudsucker Proxy* promotion kit; Cart., "*Crimewave.*" *Variety* May 22, 1985; *Crimewave* promotion kit; Robert Seidenberg, *"Miller's Crossing"*; David Edelstein, "The Neverending

Storyboard." *Village Voice* June 10, 1986; Richard T. Jameson, "What's in the Box?" *Film Comment* Sept.–Oct. 1991; Vincent Canby, "Screen: *Crimewave* Gangster-Film Spoof." *New York Times* June 6, 1985; Rick Groen, "A Filmgoer's Guide to Cliches." *Globe and Mail* July 3, 1987; Ron Base, "This Silly Summer, Even *Crimewave* Doesn't Pay." *Toronto Star* July 3, 1987.

Chapter Four

Tad Friend, "Inside the Coen Heads"; Eric Pooley, "Warped in America"; Lawrence O'Toole, "*Raising Arizona.*" *Maclean's* March 23, 1987; Rodney, Hill, "Small Things Considered: *Raising Arizona* and *Of Mice and Men.*" *Post Script: Essays in Film and the Humanities* Summer 1989; David Denby, "Bringing Up Baby." *New York* March 16, 1987; Stephen Schiff, "Raising Coen"; Franz Lidz, "Down Mean Alleys with John Goodman." *New York Times* March 8, 1998; *Raising Arizona* promotion kit; Nick Roddick, "Oh Baby!"; "Film: *Raising Arizona*, Coen Brothers Comedy." *New York Times* March 11, 1987; Leonard Klady, "Wacky Movie's Sibling Producers Hit on Hot Formula"; John Harkness, "*Raising Arizona*'s Content-Free Form"; Robert Seidenberg, "*Miller's Crossing*"; David Handelman, "The Brothers from Another Planet"; *The Big Lebowski: The Making of a Coen Brothers Film*; Kenneth M. Chanko, "Ben Barenholtz"; Joel Coen and Ethan Coen, *Raising Arizona*. St. Martin's Press, 1988; "Cage, Nicolas." *Current Biography Yearbook*; Bruce Kirkland, "Rattling His Cage." *Toronto Sunday Sun* March 15, 1987; *Barton Fink* promotion kit; "John Goodman." *The Film Encyclopedia*; Peter de Jonge, "Being the Big Guy." *New York Times Magazine* Feb 10, 1991; Rick Lyman, "Marge's Other Job, You Betcha"; "Hunter, Holly." *Current Biography Yearbook*; "Hunter, Holly." *The Film Encyclopedia*; Jack Barth, "Praising Arizona." *Film Comment* March–April 1987; Steve Daly, "High Spirits." *Entertainment Weekly* March 15, 1996; *Miller's Crossing* promotion kit; Richard Corliss, "Rootless People." *Time* March 23, 1987; Jagr., "*Raising Arizona.*" *Variety* March 4, 1987; Rick Groen, "A Wild Ride With the Coen Clan." *Globe and Mail*, 1987; Pauline Kael. *The New Yorker* April 20, 1987; David Edelstein, "I Got You, Babe." *Village Voice* March 1987; "Coen, Joel." *Current Biography Yearbook*; John Powers, "Finking It."

Chapter Five

Miller's Crossing promotion kit; Steven Levy, "Shot-by-Shot: *Miller's Crossing*." *Premiere* March 1990; Richard Harrington, "Two-Scoop Coen"; Joan Goodman, "Behind the Scenes of a Masterful Double Bill"; David Ansen, "The Coens: Partners in Crime"; "John Turturro Finks Twice." *Interview* Sept. 1990; John Harkness, "Crossing Brings Coen Brothers Back to Brooding." *Now* Oct. 4, 1990; Dashiell Hammett, *The Glass Key*. Vintage Books, 1989; John H. Richardson, "The Joel and Ethan Story"; Joel Coen and Ethan Coen, *Barton Fink & Miller's Crossing*. Faber and Faber, 1991; Bob Thompson, "Gabriel's Crossing." *Toronto Sun* Sept. 30, 1990; Jay Scott, "A Brilliant Descent Into the Depths"; Frank N. Magill, editor, *Magill's Cinema Annual 1991*. Salem Press, 1991; Gary Giddins, "Performance." *Village Voice* Sept. 25, 1990; William Preston Robertson, "What's the Goopus?" *American Film* Aug. 1991; Kenneth M. Chanko, "Ben Barenholtz"; Peter Biskind, "Joel and Ethan Coen"; "Gabriel Byrne." *The Film Encyclopedia*; Martha Southgate, "Where Has This Guy Been All This Time?" *Toronto Star* Oct. 4, 1990; Helen Dudar, "Gabriel Byrne, Bound For *Miller's Crossing*." *New York Times*; David Denby, "Hats Off." *New York* Oct. 8, 1980; "Steve Buscemi." *The Film Encyclopedia*; Rick Groen, "A Funny-Looking Guy in a Fun-Filled Job." *Globe and Mail* Sept. 30, 1998; Deirdre Kelly, "Steve Buscemi's Bleak Comedy." *Globe and Mail* Nov. 1, 1996; Kate Meyers, "The 'Lounge' Lizard." *Entertainment Weekly* March 7, 1997; Bob Thompson, "Unlikely Star." *Toronto Star* May 25, 1997; Rebecca Ascher-Walsh, "Queen Fargo"; Liam Lacey, "Actress Makes a Dynamite Debut." *Globe and Mail* Oct. 1, 1990; Lisa Schwarzbaum, "Good Guy Bad Guy Loves His Ma." *Toronto Star* Oct. 9, 1990; Robert Seidenberg, *"Miller's Crossing"*; Phoebe Hoban, "Honest John." *New York* Aug. 12, 1991; Marlaine Glicksman, "John Turturro Interviewed by Marlaine Glicksman." *Film Comment* Sept.–Oct. 1990; "Turturro, John." *International Directory of Films and Filmmakers: Actors and Actresses*, edited by Amy L. Unterburger, St. James Press, 1997; Bruce Kirkland, "Wicked Ways"; "McDormand, Frances." *The Film Encyclopedia*; "Miller's Crossing." *Rolling Stone* Oct. 4, 1990; Jim Slotek, "Changing Lanes." *Toronto Sun* March 1, 1998; Tad Friend, "Inside the Coen Heads"; David Gritten, "The Coen Mystique"; Peter Goddard, "Crooks, Molls, Mood and Music Make Gangster Tale Must-See Film." *Toronto Star* Oct. 5, 1990; Bill Brownstein, "Slick

Gangster Spoof Cracks Wise, Lacks Heart." *Montreal Gazette* Oct. 5, 1990; John Powers, "Finking It."

Chapter Six

Barton Fink promotion kit; Richard T. Jameson, "What's In the Box?"; James Wolcott, *"Barton Fink." Vanity Fair* Sept. 1991; Terrence Rafferty, "Showoffs." *New Yorker* Sept. 1991; Philip French, "A Fink on the Brink." *The Observer* Feb. 16, 1992; Franz Lidz, "Down Mean Alleys with John Goodman"; Bruce Kirkland, "Wicked Ways"; Manohla Dargis, "Double Vision." *Village Voice* Aug. 13, 1991; Michel Ciment et Hubert Nioget, "Un Rocher sur la Plage." *Positif* Sept. 1991; Jonathan Rosenbaum, "Crass Consciousness." *Chicago Reader*; Hillal Italie, *"Barton Fink* 'Weird' Says Co-Creator." *London Free Press* Aug. 24, 1991; *The Big Lebowski: The Making of a Coen Brothers Film*; William Preston Robertson, "What's the Goopus?"; *Barton Fink & Miller's Crossing*; Phoebe Hoban, "Honest John"; Craig MacInnis, "Coen Brothers Needle Hollywood in Jokey, Disturbing *Barton Fink*." *Toronto Star* Sept. 13, 1991; Brian D. Johnson, "Blank Comedy." *Maclean's* Sept. 23, 1991; John Powers, "Finking It"; Peter Travers, "What's in the Box?" *Rolling Stone* Aug. 22, 1991; "Joel Coen." *Current Biography Yearbook*; David Ansen, "Abandon Hope, All Ye Who Enter Here." *Newsweek* Aug. 26, 1991; J. Hoberman, "Hellywood." *Village Voice* Aug. 27, 1991; *Fargo* promotion kit; William Preston Robertson, "The Coen Brothers Made Easy"; *The Hudsucker Proxy* promotion kit.

Chapter Seven

Nisid Hajari, "Beavis and Egghead." *Entertainment Weekly* April 1, 1994; Jonathan Rosenbaum, "Kids' Stuff." *Chicago Reader* April 1, 1994; *Hudsucker Proxy* promotion kit; Tad Friend, "Inside the Coen Heads"; David Giammarco, "The Horror, the Horror of Sam Raimi"; Todd McCarthy, *"The Hudsucker Proxy." Variety* Jan. 31, 1994; Juliann Garey, "Coen to Extremes." *Entertainment Weekly* Feb. 5, 1993; Owen Gleiberman, "Lord of the Ring." *Entertainment Weekly* March 11, 1994; Joel Coen, Ethan Coen, and Sam Raimi, *The Hudsucker*

Proxy. Faber and Faber, 1994; Claire Bickley, "Funny Business." *Toronto Sun* March 14, 1993; Jay Scott, "New Yorkers Thirst For Coens' *Blood*"; Wolf Schneider, "Tim Lightens Up." *Coverstory* February 21, 1994; John Clark, "Strange Bedfellows." *Premiere* April 1994; *"The Hudsucker Proxy." Rolling Stone* March 24, 1994; David Gritten, "The Coen Mystique"; W.C. Odien, "The Rise and Fall of Norville Barnes." *Cinefax* June 1994; Peter Biskind, "Joel and Ethan Coen"; Richard Schickel, "Half-Baked in Corporate Hell." *Time* March 28, 1994; John Powers, "Coen South." *New York* March 14, 1994; Derek Malcolm, "The Making of a Company President." *Manchester Guardian Weekly* Sept. 11, 1994; Geoff Pevere, "All Talk, No Substance." *Globe and Mail* March 11, 1994; John Griffin, "Bugs Bunny Attitude Inspires Coen Brothers' *Hudsucker Proxy*." *Montreal Gazette* March 26, 1994; Dan Yakir, "Two Nice Boys and a Camera"; *The Big Lebowski: The Making of a Coen Brothers Film.*

Chapter Eight

Fargo promotion kit; Lizzie Francke, "Hell Freezes Over." *Sight and Sound* May 1996; "Do Not Miss *Fargo*." *The Big Lebowski: The Making of a Coen Brothers Film*; Neal Karlen, "If the Shoe (Snowshoe?) Fits, Well. . . ." *New York Times* May 5, 1996; Robert Fulford, "Cruel Irony at Heart of Coens' Fascinating Films." *Globe and Mail* March 27, 1996; Eric Pooley, "Warped in America"; Ethan Coen and Joel Coen, *Fargo*. Faber and Faber, 1996; Rick Lyman, "Marge's Other Job, You Betcha"; Dan Yakir, "Two Nice Boys and a Camera"; Bruce Weber, "So Visible He's Been Easy to Miss. Until Now." *New York Times* April 20, 1997; Liam Lacey, "William H. Macy Has Made a Deal." *Globe and Mail* Oct. 31, 1998; Chris Probst, "Cold-Blooded Scheming." *American Cinematographer* March 1996; Peter Biskind, "Joel and Ethan Coen"; Rebecca Ascher-Walsh, "Queen Fargo"; William McDonald, "Brothers in a Movie World of their Own." *New York Times* March 3, 1998; *Mr. Showbiz* web site; Jim Slotek, "Poison Pen Letter Home." *Toronto Sun* March 10, 1996; Leonard Klady, "Coens Commit Near-Perfect Crime." *Variety*; Janet Maslin, "Milquetoast's Deadly Kidnapping Plot." *New York Times* March 8, 1996; Rick Groen, "Fargo Slyly Twists American Fable." *Globe and Mail* March 22, 1996; Richard Corliss, "Swede 'n' Sour." *Time* May 13, 1996; Georgia Brown, "Only the Lonely." *Village Voice* March 12, 1996; Steven

Levy, "Shot-by-Shot: *Miller's Crossing*"; Peter Howell, "McDormand Moves On." *Toronto Star* April 9, 1997; "Coen Bros. Unmasked." *Toronto Sun* Feb. 14, 1997; Jim Slotek, "Changing Lanes"; David Gritten, "The Coen Mystique"; Simon Houpt, "A Dolt Made Good." *National Post* Nov. 28, 1998; Douglas J. Rowe, "The Coen Brothers' *Fargo*." *Brainerd Daily Dispatch*; Richard Helm, "TV *Fargo* Finds Cold Comfort in Canada." *Toronto Star* March 23, 1997.

Chapter Nine

Jonathan Romney, "In Praise of Goofing Off." *Sight and Sound* May 1998; Jim Slotek, "Changing Lanes"; Doug Stone, "The Coens Speak (Reluctantly)." *Indiewire* web site; Michel Ciment and Hubert Niogret, "Joel and Ethan Coen." *Positif* May 1998; Ethan Coen and Joel Coen, *The Big Lebowski*. Faber and Faber, 1998; *The Big Lebowski: The Making of a Coen Brothers Film*; Steven Levy, "Shot-by-Shot: *Miller's Crossing*"; Jonathan Rosenbaum, "L.A. Residential." *Chicago Reader*; Manohla Dargis, "The Brothers Freak." *L.A. Weekly*; Franz Lidz, "Down Mean Alleys With John Goodman"; David Gritten, "The Coen Mystique"; Thelma Adams, "Bowled Over!" *New York Post*; Janet Maslin "Oddballs Hurling Bowling Balls in a Setting Made for Mischief." *New York Times* March 6, 1998; J. Hoberman, "Fool's Paradise." *Village Voice* March 10, 1998; Rick Groen, "Coen Flick Like a Pinball Arcade." *Globe and Mail* March 6, 1998; Richard Schickel, "A Bit Off Their Game." *Time* March 2, 1998; Todd McCarthy, "*Big Lebowski* Has Little Appeal." *Variety* Jan. 20, 1998; Kenneth Turan, "Nutcase Noir and Geezer Noir." *Los Angeles Times*.

Chapter Ten

Raising Arizona promotion kit; email letter to author from American Conservatory Theatre, Dec. 1999; Ethan Coen, *Gates of Eden*. William Morrow, 1998; Christopher Lehman-Haupt, "Shadowy Snapshots of a Nightmare Dreamscape." *New York Times* Dec. 17, 1998.

Conclusion

Mr. Showbiz Web site and other internet sources; David Gritten, "The Coen Mystique"; Simon Houpt, "A Dolt Made Good."

Other Sources

Bruce Kirkland, "Guns, Guts 'n' Glory." *Toronto Sun* Oct. 5, 1990; Jay Scott, "Take the Money and Write." *Globe and Mail* Sept. 9, 1991; Bill Brownstein, "*Barton Fink* a Deliciously Nasty Affair." *Montreal Gazette* Sept. 13, 1991; Allen Barra, "Bat Man." *Entertainment Weekly* May 1, 1992; David Edelstein, "Invasion of the Baby Snatchers." *American Film* April 1987; "What Is a New Director?" *New York Times* March 29, 1987; "Macy, William H." *The Film Encyclopedia*; Lisa Schwarzbaum, "In Very Cold Blood." *Entertainment Weekly* March 29, 1996; Brian Lowry, "TV Networks Bank on Big Names." *Toronto Star* March 18, 1997; Judy Gerstel, "Coen Homecoming Brilliant." *Toronto Star* March 22, 1996; "Coens Win Writers Guild's Top Award." *Globe and Mail* March 18, 1997; Fred Schuers, "Nicolas Cage Is a Hollywood Samurai." *Rolling Stone* Nov. 16, 1995; Stephen Schiff, "The Movie-Maniac Cabal." *Vanity Fair* Jan. 1985; Reitinger, Douglas W., "Too Long in the Wasteland: Visions of the American West in Film, 1980–1990." *Film and History* vol. 26, no. 1, 1996; Bruce Kirkland, "The Coens Want to Bring Mayhem Right Up Front." *Toronto Sun* April 12, 1985; Mark Horowitz, "Coen Brothers A–Z." *Film Comment* Sept.–Oct. 1991.